YAHUSHUA MESSIAH, THE LAST ADAM

His humanity according to Scripture

The first man Adam was made into a living being;
the last Adam, into a life-giving spirit.
1 Corinthians 15:45

Dr Gilbert W Olson

Bride of Messiah Series, Book One

ISBN: 0986292907
ISBN 13: 9780986292903
Library of Congress Control Number: 2014922140
Gilbert Olson, Meridian, ID

Dedication
and Acknowledgements

I dedicate this book to the body of Messiah worldwide, and particularly to Key of David Christian Church, Seattle, Washington; House of David Ministries, Boise, Idaho; the assemblies in Europe, Africa, South America and the Republic of the Philippines that have chosen to come under their leadership; and the many other assemblies throughout the world that have benefited from their ministries.

I thank my wife, Beverly, and my friends Karina Casebolt and Sylvia Spencer for their encouragement to me in writing and for proofing my manuscript. I also thank my pastor, Dr. Douglas A. Morris, for his many insights that have resulted in continued improvement of the book. Most of all, I thank my Father in heaven for calling me to the ministry of being among the many who are calling the company of believers who are the bride of Messiah to get ready for the return of their Bridegroom.

Gilbert Olson

Table of Contents

Introduction to the
Bride of Messiah Series

The spirit and the bride say, "Come!" (Rev. 22:17)

Let me introduce myself. My name is Gilbert Olson. I have a rack of degree letters after my name, including Th.D., a doctorate in theology. I am an ordained minister, was a missionary in Africa and the Philippines for many years during which time I supervised and trained pastors and church leaders, have pastored churches in the United States, and was academic dean of a Scripture college. I am now retired from all those positions, but still teach in a Scripture college as well as write.

The bride of Messiah is the reason for creation, and the purpose of this series is to show, from the Scriptures, what this bride is and how those of mankind who choose to fulfill their reason for existence may become that bride. Messiah is a Hebrew title meaning a human that is anointed for a particular office, such as a king or priest.

All of Scripture, from Genesis to Revelation, is written to produce this bride. The Scriptures have no other purpose. Everything in them, every detail, has that reason.

The Creator created mankind so that he would have a people who, of their own free will, would choose to be like him in all his purity, righteousness and selfless love and thus be one with him so that he could live in them in such a way that they would show him to one another. The Scriptures call the people who choose this the bride of Messiah. This is seen in the symbol of the New Jerusalem in the last two chapters of the Book of Revelation.

We are in the last days before the return of our Messiah to establish his 1000-year rule on earth, called the Millennium. When he comes, his bride company of believers will come with him. But how did they become the bride? What qualifications did they fulfill? Just being born again is not sufficient. There is more—much, much more.

In this series we follow the major rules for interpreting Scripture.

1) The Scriptures—Genesis to Revelation—are the inspired word of Elohim (God/Strong One), and therefore are the *only* source of authority. This means church tradition and creeds have no authority for anything.

2) Let Scripture interpret Scripture. This means church tradition and creeds must not be used to interpret Scripture.

3) Words must mean what they mean. This means church tradition and creeds must not be used to change the meaning of words.

The first in this series is titled "Yahushua Messiah, The Last Adam." This is the first, for it shows from Scripture that he is a man, and man means human only, not a god-man. This was the belief at the time of Messiah and the early assembly (church). The god-man belief didn't officially come into the church until the Council of Nicea in 325 C.E. (Common Era) by which time there was much compromise with paganism. It was this belief that rejected the monotheism (belief in one God who is one only) of the Old Testament, mixed it with polytheism (belief in many gods), and introduced a false monotheism called the Trinity (three Gods, called Persons, in one Essence—each a separate identity, yet each the whole of the Essence).

In these writings I use some special words. It is my hope that by doing so these words will help you understand things on a deeper level, and perhaps also from a different point of view.

Our English language is full of words that have their roots in paganism. And these words, by natural consequence, are in the assembly. Why? Because we use language to convey or communicate ideas, and so we communicate in words people understand. But, in order to understand *our* subject, I use different words. Here is a list of words you will meet.

Those who wish to confirm the following usages are encouraged to do their own research. The internet has numerous articles on all of them. But don't settle for just one source. Look at many and dig deep. Often the surface definition is from tradition.

1. Elohim (eh-low-HEEM). Elohim is a Hebrew word that is most often translated as "God" or "gods." These English words have to do with supernatural beings, such as deity or godness. In fact, the English word God comes from the pre-Christian German sky-god Gott. But Elohim doesn't mean this. It means "Strong One" or "strong ones," depending on the context. Although it most often refers to our Father, the creator of all, it also refers to humans and angels. A judge in the Old Testament, for example, is sometimes referred to as *elohim*. In fact, Elohim himself refers to us humans as *elohim*. That's in Psalm 82:6. Other forms of Elohim are *El* and *Eloah*. El is often used as part of a person's name. For example, Nathaniel means "gift of Elohim."

2. Yahuah (yah-HOO-ah). Yahuah is the personal name of Elohim. The Hebrew letters for this name (in English) are YHWH. You may be familiar with Jehovah and Yahweh as transliterations of these letters. Many, including me, believe that Yahuah is the correct spelling.

The name Yahuah has a meaning, as with most Hebrew names. It means "He is." He is the self-existing one. In Exodus 3:15 Yahuah told Moses that this is his name forever and he is to be remembered by this name for all generations. And it was used for many centuries. The Old Testament has it over 6000 times and his name was continually on the lips of the people. But when the Southern Kingdom of Judah was taken into captivity by the Babylonians, called the Babylonian Captivity, things changed. They stopped using his name. They even came to believe that it was blasphemy to speak his name. So they used a substitute title instead: they used Adonai.

Adonai is a Hebrew word meaning Master or Lord. In fact, that is the practice of the Jews today when they read the Old Testament in Hebrew. Wherever *YHWH* appears, they say Adonai instead of Yahuah.

This practice has come into our English translations. So whenever you see LORD all in capital letters, it is not a translation (which means translating the meaning of a word into a different language), nor a transliteration (which means translating the letters of one language into another but not giving the meaning). Rather it is a substitution, a replacement. It is changing the word of Elohim into something different from what he inspired to be written. Proverbs 30:6 and Revelation 22:18-19 condemn this practice.

Yah is a shortened form of Yahuah, and is often used as part of a person's name. An example is Elijah. In Hebrew it is Eliyahu: My Elohim is Yahuah. Another example of "yah" is the much used word halleluyah. It means praise Yahuah.

3. Yahushua (yah-hoo-SHOO-ah). This is the Hebrew name of our Savior. It means Yahuah is salvation, or Yahuah the savior. The English name "Jesus" wasn't known until about 500 years ago when the letter "J" was invented. Before then it was Yesus. But even that is a migration from Hebrew into Greek (Ieseus), then into Latin (Iesus), and finally into English. By saying the name Yahushua we are saying the name of his Father, Yahuah, and that he is our savior.

4. Messiah. This is a Hebrew word meaning anointed one. Kings and priests were anointed when they came into office. The Greek equivalent is *christos*, or Christ, which also means anointed one, but this Greek word comes from paganism.

4. Master. This is a better translation than the word Lord. The source of the word Lord/lord is from paganism.

5. Assembly. This is a better translation than the word church. The Greek word *ekklesía*, commonly translated as church, means assembly. The English word "church" comes from the name of the Greek goddess Kirke. She was a goddess who turned people into pigs and other animals. Worshipers of Kirke met in a circular building. Words beginning with cir-, such as circle, circus, circumcision, circumnavigate, etc., come from the name of this goddess.

6. Set-apart. This is a better translation than the word holy. Holy is a religious word from paganism. Both the Hebrew and Greek words translated as holy have as their root meaning separation. Something or a person can be set-apart on the positive side to the true Elohim, or on the negative side to the false ones.

7. Favor. This is a better translation than the word grace. Grace is a religious word from paganism. Both the Hebrew and Greek words translated as grace mean favor, particularly undeserved favor.

8. Esteem. This is a better translation than the word glory. Again, glory is a religious word from paganism. The root meaning of the Hebrew and Greek words translated as glory is weight. Metaphorically, it means the weight of honor or esteem or splendor.

9. Yisra'el. This spelling is closer to Hebrew than Israel. The apostrophe in it indicates that originally they pronounced a break between the two letters. Today, however, they elide over that break. Yisra'el was the grandson of Abraham, although he originally was named Ya'aqov (Jacob). Yisra'el means "he who struggles with Elohim" or "prince of Elohim." He got this name when he struggled with an angel of Elohim. You can read the story in Genesis 32:28.

Okay, so much for vocabulary.

In writing this series my desire is that lives—your life—may be changed, that you may find an ever deepening relationship with Yahuah your Father and with Yahushua Messiah his son. For this you were created. Life on earth is the preparation for life with them for eternity: *What you have become* at the end of your temporary life on this earth *is what you begin with* in your permanent life on the new earth. It is forever.

Preface

"Is there not a cause?" 1Sa 27:29 (KJV)

When I told a pastor friend that I was attending Bible college classes at a certain assembly, he warned me that they were a cult because they didn't believe in the Trinity. At that time I had just begun attending and couldn't answer him except to say, "The Bible says God is one, not three-in-one." He challenged me to pray about it, as I did him.

That night as I lay on my bed I prayed, "God, are you one or three in one? I don't care which, I just want to be right." He answered immediately and powerfully in my mind. I will never forget it. **"IN MY WORD I SAID I AM ONE!"**

I was rebuked. I felt like I was being pushed through the mattress onto the floor and then squeezed through a knot hole! I said, "I believe. Help me to understand properly the verses that Trinitarians use to support their belief in the Trinity." The following years of going through the entire Bible in that college gave me the understanding that I could build on. But there was more to learn. What about the dual nature of Christ, that he is a God-man, 100% deity as the Father is and 100% humanity as we are? To that I had no answer.

In 1984 the pastor of that assembly sent my wife and me to the Philippines to begin an assembly and Bible school. Soon we had an assembly and my reputation (or should I say "notoriety") spread throughout the Charismatic ministries in that nation. "Horrors! He is baptizing in the name of Jesus! He is a cult! Stay away from him!" I was doing what the apostles did in the Book of Acts, and that made me a cult!

Two years later I started a Bible school and began preparing the class material. That material included explaining the nature of God and his son. Then it hit me: "Words must mean what they mean." This is a primary rule of understanding any writing. It is the foundation rule that when Elohim says he is one, he means a numerical one and not a "three-in-one, one-in-three trinity." It is the rule that Elohim pressed me with on my bed when I prayed about his nature. This rule also applies to his only begotten son, Yahushua. Scripture calls him a man, and man means man only. *"God was **in** Christ reconciling the world to himself"* (2Cor 5:19), not God **was** Christ. This revelation led me to write a booklet that I titled *God in Man*.

After leaving the Philippines in 1997 I began enlarging that booklet, and in 2005 I adapted it to be used as a Scripture college textbook. In 2014, after several people had asked for copies of it, I realized the information in it needed to be rewritten into a book for the general public. So this book has been a work in progress for 28 years, with many insights added during those years. Included in those added insights are changes in vocabulary by using the Hebrew names and words for Elohim and his son.

Trinitarians are the vast majority orthodox: orthodox meaning church tradition based on man-made creeds.[1] The first Trinitarian related creed was in 325 C.E. at the Council of Nicea, and belief in it was enforced by the Roman emperor Constantine.

Non-trinitarians are the smaller minority. There are many disagreements in Christendom. Believing that Elohim is one and not a Trinity and that Yahushua is a man and not a god-man—the position of this book—is one of them.

The orthodox Trinitarian belief is so entrenched in the church that it has come to define what Christianity is and sets it apart from all other religions. In contrast, this book presents the man Yahushua Messiah as

---

1 Orthodox: Conforming to the Christian faith as represented in the creeds of the early church. (Random House Kernerman Webster's College Dictionary.)

what *Scripture* says Christianity is supposed to be and sets it apart from all other religions.

May the reader be blessed.
Gilbert Olson

Scriptures quotations are from the following versions, all used by permission. Words in brackets and emphases added. If there is no source citation it is my own translation from Hebrew or Greek after having done comparisons with various translations and also using Hebrew and Greek dictionaries and lexicons.

CJB = Complete Jewish Bible
NAS = the New American Standard Bible
NASU = the New American Standard Bible Update
NIV = the New International Version
NKJV = the New King James Version
NRS = New Revised Standard Version
TLB = The Living Bible
TS = The Scriptures

The Scripture book abbreviations are as follows:

Gen-Genesis	1Ki-1 Kings	Ecc-Ecclesiastes	Ob-Obadiah
Ex-Exodus	2Ki-2 Kings	SS-Song of Songs	Jon-Jonah
Le-Leviticus	1Ch-1 Chronicles	Is-Isaiah	Mi-Micah
Nu-Numbers	2Ch-2 Chronicles	Jer-Jeremiah	Na-Nahum
Dt-Deuteronomy	Ezr-Ezra	Lam-Lamentations	Hab-Habakkuk
Jos-Joshua	Ne-Nehemiah	Eze-Ezekiel	Ze-Zephaniah
Jdg-Judges	Est-Esther	Dan-Daniel	Hag-Haggai
Ru-Ruth	Job-Job	Ho-Hosea	Zec-Zechariah
1Sa-1 Samuel	Ps-Psalms	Joel-Joel	Mal-Malachi
2Sa-2 Samuel	Pr-Proverbs	Am-Amos	
Mt-Matthew	2Cor-2Corinthians	1Ti-1 Timothy	2Pe-2 Peter
Mk-Mark	Gal-Galatians	2Ti-2 Timothy	1Jn-1 John
Lk-Luke	Eph-Ephesians	Tit-Titus	2Jn-2 John
Jn-John	Php-Philippians	Phm-Philemon	3Jn-3 John
Ac-Acts	Col-Colossians	Heb-Hebrews	Jude-Jude
Ro-Romans	1Th-1 Thess.	Jam-James	Rev-Revelation
1Cor-1Corinthians	2Th-2 Thess.	1Pe-1 Peter	

PART ONE: THE MAN

CHAPTER ONE

Introduction

———∞∞∞———

IT TAKES A RADICAL CHANGE TO MOVE from the Trinitarian belief that God is a God-essence (or Godhead) of three separate Persons (each the whole Essence yet each different from the other) to what the Scriptures say, that he is one (Dt 6:4; Gal 3:20; etc.). Many of you reading this will be seeing ideas different from what you are used to. So please be patient. It is my hope that as we go along, eventually your questions will be answered.

The Christian faith began by having its foundation on the Old Testament, a Hebrew book. This was the Scriptures used at the time of Yahushua and the early assembly. The OT writers wrote in Hebrew (with a little bit of Aramaic), and the NT writers, although writing in Greek, did so according to their Hebrew culture and thinking. This thinking is very different from our Western thinking, a thinking with its roots in Greek culture.

In fact, we believers in Messiah are spiritual Jews. We have been adopted as sons of Elohim through Yahushua Messiah (Ro 11:6-8. Eph 1:5). We need to understand our faith through the *eyes* of Hebrew thinking as seen in Scripture. This is what Yahuah inspired to be written and he did it through their culture.

> "For my thoughts are not your thoughts,
> Nor are my ways my ways," declares Yahuah.
> "For as the heavens are higher than the earth,
> So are my ways higher than your ways
> And my thoughts than your thoughts."
> (Is 55:8-9)

Hebrew thinking.[1]

In Hebrew, as noted earlier, there is no word for deity, although *elohim* is used for it. In the KJV, *elohim* is translated with these definitions:

> God 2346, god 244, judge 5, GOD 1, goddess 2, great 2, mighty 2, angels 1, exceeding 1, God-ward + 04136 1, godly 1; 2606. • 1) (plural) 1a) rulers, judges 1b) divine ones 1c) angels 1d) gods 2) (plural intensive - singular meaning) 2a) god, goddess 2b) godlike one 2c) works or special possessions of God 2d) the (true) God 2e) God.[2]

The shortened form of *elohim* is *el.* In the KJV it is translated with these definitions as follows, emphasis added:

> God 213, god 16, power 4, mighty 5, goodly 1, great 1, idols 1, **Immanuel** + 06005 2, might 1, strong 1; 245 • 1) god, god-like one, mighty one 1a) mighty men, men of rank, mighty heroes 1b) angels 1c) god, false god, (demons, imaginations) 1d) God, the one true God, Jehovah 2) mighty things in nature 3) strength, power.[3]

It is context that determines how a word is used, not the word by itself. An example is Immanuel. Common English versions translate it as "God with us," meaning, "Deity with us." But it doesn't mean that. It can mean "a mighty one with us" or "a magistrate with us," or "a representative of the Creator with us," or, as we shall see later, "the mighty one's nature with us."

Why, in Hebrew thinking, is there no word for deity? Is not deity important to them? Yes, it is important—it is the center of their culture. But they don't think of deity the way we Western (Grecian/Hellenistic) thinkers do. The contrast is static thinking versus dynamic thinking. Western thinking regarding deity is philosophical, wanting to know what

---

1 The World Wide Web has many articles on the differences between Greek and Hebrew thinking. The reader is encouraged to look them up.

2 Strong's #0430, BibleWorks database.

3 Strong's #0410, BibleWorks database.

it is and how to categorize it. Hebrew thinking wants to know what he does and what he expects of us. "God" is a static word of being; *elohim* is a dynamic word of action—someone or thing that is strong is doing something.

An example is the battle on Mount Carmel in which Elijah challenged the people as to who is **the** strong one *[elohim]*. Is it Yahuah, or is it the Ba'al.[4]

> Elijah went before the people and said, "How long will you waver between two opinions? If Yahuah is **the** strong one, follow him; but if **the** Ba'al, follow him." (1Ki 18:21)

When the prophets of the Ba'al couldn't get their strong one to send fire to burn the sacrifice, Elijah prayed to his strong one:

> "Answer me, Yahuah, answer me, so these people will know that you, Yahuah, are **the** strong one, and that you are turning their hearts back again." Then the fire of Yahuah fell and burned up the sacrifice, the wood, the stones and the soil, and also licked up the water in the trench. When all the people saw this, they fell prostrate and cried, "Yahuah! He is **the** strong one! Yahuah! He is **the** strong one!" (1Ki 18:37-39)

Another aspect of Hebrew thinking is the value of names. In Western thinking, names are static, like Bob or Gilbert. They are used as labels to identify people and things. I have asked people if they know the meaning of their names. Few do. I looked up my name, Gilbert. It means bright. But to me it is only a label. My parents chose it not for its meaning but because they liked it.

In contrast, Hebrew names tell a story. When parents name their child, they do so according to the circumstances of the birth, or according to what they want their child to become, or even prophetically of what he will do. An example is Elijah. The Hebrew is *Eliyahu [el-ee-YAH-hoo]*. *El* means *strong one*, as we have seen. The letter *i* when added to

---

4 The definite article is in the Hebrew, but not in English translations.

a noun is the possessive pronoun *my.* So the name Eli means *my strong one. Yahu* is an abbreviation of *Yahuah,* the name of the strong one. So Eliyahu means *my strong one is Yahuah.* This is what we saw in the confrontation on Mount Carmel and in his whole ministry. His name represents his ministry. To the Hebrew, when you say Eliyahu, you have in mind all he did. Another example is Elisha [el-ee-SHA], the successor of Eliyahu. *Sha* means salvation. So his name means *my strong one is salvation.* As with Eliyahu, we can see this meaning in Elisha's ministry.

Not only does a name tell a story, it also describes character. Both Eliyahu and Elisha lived the meaning of their names. Most people don't, even though their names have great meaning. But these two did, as well as many other people of *the strong one.*

The strong one himself has a name, one he gave himself, a name of profound meaning, a name which describes his character and what he did, still does and will do. **That name is Yahuah.** It means *he is.* It is a name of self-existence, a name of being eternal without beginning or end, a name of absolute power to accomplish all he wishes, a name of knowing everything past, present and future, a name of being everything we need him to be, a name of faithfulness to accomplish all he says, a name of compassion, love and mercy, a name of righteousness and justice, a name of set-apartness from all that is against his nature of goodness and love, commonly called holiness. This last aspect includes all his moral attributes. He is the spirit of set-apartness (holiness).

All of these aspects are seen throughout Scripture, and especially in the Book of Psalms. Each aspect of the name is something he did or promises to do or appealed to in prayer. When the Jews used the name it recalled their history of mighty power in which he released them from captivity in Egypt, destroyed the Egyptian army in the sea, led them through the wilderness 40 years, gave them the Promised Land, and gave them David as their king. Their whole history and their promised future is in that name. His name and what he did is the center of their culture—they are spiritually minded.

Yahuah combines his name with activities to show the kind of strong one he is. Here is a partial list. Each has an historical context with spiritual applications for those who follow him.

Yahuah-yireh: Yahuah sees (to it; i.e. provides) (Gen 22:14). Abraham gave this name to Mount Moriah when Yahuah provided a ram when he was about to slay his son as an offering to Yahuah. Years later on Mount Moriah, Yahuah gave his son Yahushua to die for our sins.

Yahuah-nissi: Yahuah is my banner (in battle) (Ex 17:15). Moses gave this name to an altar he built after Yahuah had given them victory over the army of Amalek.

Yahuah-shalom: Yahuah is peace (Jdg 6:24). Gideon gave this name to an altar he built after Yahuah commissioned him to defeat Midian. He was afraid because of seeing the angel face to face, so Yahuah said to him, *"Peace to you, do not fear; you shall not die."*

Yahuah-tsaba'ot: Yahuah of armies (Almighty, NIV; of hosts, KJV) (1Sa 1:3). This is a frequent term in Scripture showing Yahuah as the commander of the armies of heaven.

Yahuah-meqadishkem: Yahuah who sets you apart (who makes you holy, NIV; who sanctifies you, NAS). Yahuah gave sabbath-keeping as a sign that *"I am Yahuah who sets you apart"* (Ex 31:13).[5]

Yahuah-ro'i: Yahuah is my shepherd (Ps 23:1). Without the possessive *my* (*i*), it is **Yahuah-ra'ah.** Some know it as Jehovah Ra'ah.)

Yahuah-ropheka: *"I am Yahuah who heals you"* (Ex 15:26). Without the object pronoun *you* (*ka*), it is **Yahuah-rapha.** Yahuah promised this blessing to those who obey his commandments.

Yahuah-tsidkenu: Yahuah our righteousness (Jer 23:6). This is prophetic of Messiah who has become to us from Elohim *"righteousness and set-apartness and redemption"* (1Cor 1:30).

Yahuah-shammah: Yahuah is there (Eze 48:45). This name is prophetic of Yahuah's personal presence in the millennial kingdom, and also in us who believe in his son, Yahushua.

Yahuah Elohim Yisra'el: Yahuah, the Strong One of Yisra'el (Jdg 5:3; Is 17:6). This is a frequent phrase in Scripture. It shows his relationship to Yisra'el (and believers in Messiah) in contrast to the false strong ones of the gentiles (unbelievers in Messiah).

---

5 Yahushua is the fulfillment of that sign. When we obey him, we are observing sabbath. The OT has many sabbaths, not just the 7th day.

Yahuah Eloheka El Qana: Yahuah your Strong One is a jealous Strong One (Ex 20:5; Dt 5:9). As a husband wants total faithfulness from his wife, so Yahuah wants total faithfulness from his people. Unfaithfulness is sin and results in judgment.

Besides these descriptive names of Yahuah there are descriptive titles of Elohim. It is good to look up the context of each. **El Olam:** The Strong One of eternity (Gen 21:33). **El Shaddai:** The Strong One Almighty (Gen 17:1). **El Elyon:** The Strong One Most High (Gen 14:18).

With this Hebrew thinking of "name" in mind, we will look again at the name Immanuel. *"The pregnant virgin will give birth to a son and call his **name** Immanuel* (Is 7:14). Wait! In a dream the angel told Joseph to call his name Yahushua, for he shall save his people from their sins (Mt 1:21). The name Yahushua means Yahuah the Savior. No one ever called him Immanuel. Is this a contradiction? Did the angel forget the prophetic name in Isaiah and give a different one? No one thinks that. In the same dream the angel said the reason for the name Yahushua was to fulfill the prophecy to call his name Emmanuel.[6] This means "call his **character** Elohim with us." Yahushua said, *"He who has seen me has seen the Father"* (Jn 14:9). When you see the man Yahushua, you see the character of our creator Yahuah. Paul wrote the same thing of Messiah: *"He is the image of the invisible Elohim."* (Col 1:15).[7]

We now look at the word *spirit.* The Hebrew word is *ruach.* Strong's definition gives a wide variety of meanings, one of which is very telling: "as seat especially of moral character."[8] "Ruach Studies" in "Hebrew Streams" says this, emphasis added:

> God's Ruach/Heart/Mind could be called his resident disposition, character, or **nature**. This nature he wants implanted in Israel (and all human beings) to remold them, rebirth them, recreate

---

6 Mt 1:23. Emmanuel is the Greek transliteration of the Hebrew Immanuel.

7 The Greek uses *theos* to translate *Elohim*. See also Heb 1:3, *"the exact representation of His nature"* NAS.

8 Strong's #7307, BibleWorks database.

them with his "new" character, in his image. In his "image" was the original intent (Gen 1:26).[9]

Yahuah's spirit is his nature, just as his name represents his nature. His nature or character is not a third person of deity. Such an idea is totally foreign, alien, to Hebrew thinking. The idea of his spirit being a Person of deity is repugnant. It is from Greek philosophical mythological paganism. It has no place in the body of Messiah. Expunge it from your thinking and soul like the spiritual poison it is if you have it. This book is written to be an antidote to help you do that and to help others do that.

This information of Hebrew thinking applies to what Yahushua commanded us to do after his resurrection.

Is given to me all authority in heaven and upon the earth. You go therefore, disciple all the nations, immersing them into the character of the Father and of the son and of the spirit of set-apartness.[10]

The word *holy* is an adjective. It means set-apart. Messiah did not—repeat, did not—give these words to be a formula to say when immersing believers in water. The Book of Acts shows they never ever used those words as something to say. Rather than saying the words, they obeyed the words by training converts to be like the Father and the son in their characters, which is the spirit of set-apartness. It is a spiritual immersion. In the NT we see immersion in water, in fire, in the spirit and in the name.

The Book of Revelation mentions seven spirits of Elohim and that Yahushua has them.[11] Isaiah prophesied that the Messiah would have these seven spirits and lists them. All are character traits of Yahuah. They are not Persons of deity.

And shall rest upon him spirit of Yahuah, spirit of wisdom and of understanding, spirit of counsel and of might, spirit of knowledge and of fear of Yahuah. (Is 11:2)

---

9 http://www.hebrew-streams.org/works/spirit/ruachpneuma.html.

10 Mt 28:19, Greek word order.

11 Rev 1:4; 3:1; 4:5; 5:6.

Both the Father and son have personal names, but what describes the spirit is an adjective—set-apart from the things of the world (selfishness and darkness) to the things of the Father (selfless love and light). Yahuah's spirit is the spirit of set-apartness. It is not a person to have a personal name. The job of the body of Messiah (commonly called church) is to get converts and train them to be like Messiah, separate from all sin and fully obedient to Messiah so they can be lights to the world of what Yahuah created us to be. Our goal as believers is that when people see us, they see past us to Messiah, and through him to see Yahuah. This is the bride of Messiah.

A final word we need to look at to understand Hebrew thinking before moving on is "belief" or "faith." The verb is believe. Again we see the difference between the static Greek philosophical, intellectual thinking and the dynamic Hebrew action thinking. The whole testimony of Scripture is that belief without action is dead.[12] Yahushua said, *"If you love me, you will obey what I command"* (Jn 14:15). A true believer is active in promoting the kingdom of Messiah because of love. In Hebrew thinking, only he who acts believes. He who says he believes but does not act on his belief is a hypocrite, a false believer.

What happened?

Much has been lost in understanding the Scriptures after the first century. This was when pagan gentile Greek philosophers who, after converting to Christianity and becoming leaders and bishops, brought their pagan beliefs into the church and rejected everything Jewish, including the monotheism of Judaism. Originally Christianity (or "the Way")[13] was another sect of Judaism,[14] but these educated gentiles made it into a separate religion with many pagan ideas and practices. This is syncretism, uniting opposing or opposite ideas into a new idea.

Have you ever wondered why the church of today is so far different from the first century assembly? Where is the separation from the ways of

---

12 Jam 2:14-26.

13 Ac 24:14.

14 Judaism has many sects. For example, the Pharisees were a sect.

the world, called holiness? Where are the signs and wonders and miracle healings we see in the Gospels and Acts? Did Elohim change? *"I Yahuah do not change"* (Mal 3:6). Did Yahushua change? *"Yahushua Messiah is the same yesterday and today and forever"* (Heb 13:8).

But what happened? The history of the assembly after the first century is one of compromise with paganism and the ways of the world. Is there no wonder that miracle power has left? The absence of miracle power is evidence that Yahuah has withdrawn his presence. But in these last days before Messiah's return his presence is returning with the evidence of miracles.

The story line seen in the Scriptures is that of Yahuah creating man, man having intimate fellowship with him, man out of fellowship with him because of sin, and man restored to fellowship through a special man—the man Yahushua Messiah. This man ties the whole of Scripture together. Without understanding him, that he is a man and man means human only and not a god-man, and that Elohim is one and not three-in-one, and his spirit is himself, it is impossible to understand Yahuah and why he created us.

> For there is one Elohim and one mediator between Elohim and men, the **man** Messiah Yahushua, who gave himself as a ransom for all men—the testimony given in its proper time. (1Ti 2:5-6)

> For us there is but **one Elohim, the Father**, from whom all things came and for whom we live; and there is but one Master Yahushua Messiah, through whom all things came and through whom we live. (1Cor 8:6)

From time to time in this book I make negative comments regarding the doctrines of the dual nature of Christ and the Trinity, that these doctrines are not from Scripture (and therefore not from Yahuah) but are deception from our enemy, Satan, the father of lies. These negative comments are not intended to demean those who believe them, but rather to help them come out of their deception by showing how foolish and against reason they are. I am for those who believe in them. I love them so much that I am writing this book to help them understand what

Scripture really says and how against the Scriptures the orthodox belief is. To be against the Scriptures is to be against the one who inspired them.

At the time of Yahushua (and even today) the traditions of Judaism had more authority than the Scriptures. So it is in Christianity today. Because he exposed the wickedness of their traditions, they killed him. But he still loved them, and some of them repented after Pentecost.

Elohim does not judge us for ignorance of sin. (Praise Yah!) The Trinitarians I know (I grew up among them) love Jesus and want to serve him. But when I saw the truth I chose to come out of that deception. Some do, most don't.

Nowhere in Scripture is belief in the nature of God and his son connected to salvation, so it is not a salvation issue. But what we believe about it does affect how we live our Christian lives.

Before ending this introduction I need to talk about Yahushua being a "mere man." The NIV uses the term "mere man" in John 10:33 and Romans 2:3. "Mere" is not in the Greek; it is commentary. A woman asked me, "With Yahushua doing all that he did—the miracles and all, the virgin birth, living without sin—how can he be just a mere man?" What she meant was, "How can he be a human only?" **That's the point of this book.** "Mere man" means man only without any divinity—a very exceptional man, but still a human only. Scriptures are very clear, as you will see. Yahushua is a man only with no more deity than you, I or any other human.

Some think, however, that to call him a man only is degrading. They think he has to be *more* than a man only. I believe the problem lies in not understanding the distance and magnitude between what it means for the Father to be infinite Elohim and for the son to be finite human.

So, for you who might be having difficulty with the phrase "man only," I ask you, if Yahushua is not a man only, then what is he? Is he more than human? If so, then he's not human at all. Is someone who did an heroic deed more than a human only? Is a football star more than a human only? Or are all such notables just ordinary people who did unusual things?

And what about Adam? Was not he a man only before he sinned? That's what Yahushua is. He is an ordinary person, a man like Adam before he sinned, a man who did very unusual things, things which make the way for the rest of us, if we so choose, to also be unusual and do unusual things.

Now that you are introduced to the subject, we begin by looking at why Yahuah created man. Be prepared to understand more deeply the universe of reality according to Scripture.

CHAPTER TWO

The Reason Became Flesh

———❦———

In the beginning was the **reason**, and the **reason** was with Elohim, and the **reason** was Elohim. **It** was with Elohim in the beginning. Through **it** all things were made; without **it** nothing was made that has been made. In **it** was life, and that life was the light of men. ... The **reason** became flesh and lived among us. (Jn 1:1-4,14)

He is the image of the invisible Elohim. (Col 1:15)

One is Elohim and one is the mediator between Elohim and mankind, **the man** Messiah Yahushua. (1Ti 2:5)

THE ABOVE SCRIPTURE VERSES HAVE TRANSLATIONS AND vocabulary unfamiliar to most. But they are necessary to tell the story of the most wonderful and unusual man in all of human history. He is the perfect man, the man who never sinned, the man who always obeyed his Father, obeying him out of love for him and for mankind, the man who is the means whereby we, sinful mankind, can be reconciled to and have eternal fellowship with our creator.

In John 1:1-4 the common translations use "Word" (with a capital W) to translate the Greek *logos*. And they use the pronoun "He" to refer to it as a Person. The only other place some translations capitalize "word" is in Revelation 19:13: *"His name is called the Word of God."* Everywhere else they don't capitalize "word" because they know it refers to something spoken or written. They capitalize "Word" in John 1 because they believe it is an appellation or title for Christ and that he existed as God before creation, that he was co-creator with the Father, and that he would also become a man through the virgin Mary and thus would be a God-man.

So what is *logos*? It means reason, plan and thought, and the words and actions which result from that reasoning, planning and thinking. Strong's Greek-Hebrew Dictionary #3056 defines it thus:

logos (log'-os); from NT:3004 [*lego* to say]; something said (including the thought); by implication a topic (subject of discourse), also reasoning (the mental faculty) or motive; by extension, a computation.

In the New Testament *logos* never means a god, or a god-man, or Yahushua, or Christ. John was Hebrew. Although he used the Greek word *logos*, his thinking would be the Hebrew word *dābār*,[1] meaning "word, speech, matter." In the phrase "the word of Elohim (the word of God)," *logos* indicates his thoughts and will.[2] In the New Testament *logos* always means the thought or the thought expressed; it never means a person. Only in John 1:1 and in Revelation 19:13 do Trinitarian translators capitalize it to mean a Person.

This is why in John 1:1 I translated *logos* as "reason" and not "word." Yahuah exists apart from time. He created time, and from eternity past sees all the history of mankind from creation to eternity future. This is from our time-bound, finite perspective, because for him there is no eternity past: he is. Yahuah is an amazing being. On the basis of our history that he sees, he created us. The focus of our (mankind's) history is the man Yahushua who ministered about 4000 years after creation. Everything Yahuah does is according to the life of this man. Without this man there would have been no creation and this universe would not exist. This man is the reason for creation.

The apostle John was a Jew. He thought like a Jew. He knew the Scriptures (which at that time were only the Old Testament). He knew that Elohim, the creator of heaven and earth, was one in nature. He also knew that the prophesied Messiah would be a man, not a god-man. He gave the reason for his writing with these words at the end of his Gospel.

---

1 Strong's #1697. *dābār* (dah-VAHR, the underlined b is pronounced as a v).

2 Vine's Expository Dictionary of Biblical Words, Copyright © 1985, Thomas Nelson Publishers.

These have been written so that you might believe that Yahushua is the Messiah, the son of Elohim, and that believing you might possess life in his name. (Jn 20:31)

Although he wrote in Greek, his thinking was Hebrew. Throughout the whole New Testament Yahushua is always referred to as a man, never as the creator God and never as a god-man. (Later we will examine verses that Trinitarians use to show otherwise and see that their interpretations are false.)

And the prophecies in the Old Testament about the coming Messiah were always about a man, never as the creator God and never as a god-man. An example is what Moses prophesied: *"Yahuah your Elohim will raise up for you a prophet like me from among your own brothers"* (Dt 18:15). It should be noted that Moses was a man, not a god-man.

As noted earlier, the god-man doctrine, and the Trinity doctrine that came from it, are pagan. At the time of Yahushua the Pharisees believed the Talmud and Oral Law had absolute authority over the written Scripture.[3] As it was between Yahushua and the Jewish establishment, so it is now between what the New Testament says and what the Christian establishment says; it is the conflict between truth and tradition.

A look at the life of Yahushua shows us what Yahuah created us fellow humans to be. Yahushua is called the last Adam. We begin with his birth. Along the way we will compare him with the first man Adam.

So it is written: "The first man Adam became a living being"; the last Adam, a life-giving spirit. ... The first man was of the dust of the earth, **the second man from heaven**. (1Cor 15:45,47, NIV, emphasis added.)

From heaven.

What does "from heaven" mean? Trinitarians say it means one of the Three Persons that make up the essence of deity[4] traveled from

---

3 "The Hebrew Yeshua vs. the Greek Jesus" by Nehemia Gordon, pp. 83 ff.

4 "Person: Christianity. Any of the three separate individualities of the Father, Son, and Holy Spirit, as distinguished from the **essence** of the Godhead that unites them." (American Heritage Dictionary, emphasis added)

heaven to earth and changed from being all of infinite deity to become a finite human while still being all of infinite deity—a god-man. But that can't be. Besides being contrary to reason, it violates Scripture that says Elohim is one and that Yahushua is a man.

So what is this verse saying? Let's look again at what Paul wrote in First Corinthians. He said this was a *man* from heaven, not a god from heaven. Even Trinitarians don't believe Yahushua was a human in heaven before he was born on earth. In their teaching, the time that the second person of deity-essence/godhead became a human was when he was conceived in Mary's womb.

Heaven means many things, depending upon the context. It can mean the physical sky of air, clouds, sun, moon and stars. It can mean where Elohim lives and to Elohim himself. It is also used metaphorically for things related to him, such as his authority.

These verses (1Cor 15:45,47) show a contrast between two humans. The body of the first man, Adam, was of the dust of the earth with a soul and spirit. He was created perfect with no weakness or tendency toward pride and selfishness, which is sin. But when he sinned, something happened to both his body and soul. His body was changed so that it would eventually die. *"The sinning being will die"* (Eze 18:4). *"It is laid up for men to die once, and after that, judgment"* (Heb 9:27). *"The wages of sin is death"* (Ro 6:23).

We have inherited this.

Adam's soul (his being) was also modified. Before, he had unbroken relationship with Elohim by means of his spirit. He didn't need a conscience (the knowledge of good and evil) because his Father would tell him everything he needed to know when it was needed, including when not to do something he thought about doing.

When Adam sinned, that relationship was broken; he no longer had direct inward communication from Elohim. By eating from that tree of the knowledge of good and evil his soul was modified to have a conscience. This conscience would tell him when not to do something. It is a faulty guide, however. The conscience can be hardened by disobeying it. It is also damaged by one's culture, both in the family and in the society in general.

We see this all around us. If a child is born into a family in which casual sex and adultery is the norm, for example, he will likely see nothing wrong with it. The same would apply to drunkenness, drugs, domestic abuse, gang warfare and even murder. In West Africa where I lived, stealing was considered wrong if it was from the same tribe, but not wrong if it was from a different tribe.

We know how *physical* traits are passed from parents to child. We don't know how *non*-physical traits are passed. **Scripture shows us, however, that the trait of the tendency to sin is passed from the father alone.** In the New Testament this weakness is called "flesh" (Mt 26:41; Ro 6:19). We can call it the flesh nature.[5]

Numbers 14:18 says Yahuah brings the guilt of the fathers upon the sons to the third and fourth generations. Note: It is *father* to sons. This agrees with the Hebrew practice of inheritance which is also from father to sons. An example of this is the genealogies of Yahushua in Mt 1:1-17 and Lk 3:23-38. It is always from father to son.

It is logical, therefore, to conclude that as a result of what Adam did the tendency to sin (which is in the soul along with conscience) is passed on through the father.

It was after Adam sinned and was driven out of the Paradise of Eden that he had his first son, called Cain. Cain loved his own way rather than Yahuah's. Next was his brother Abel who loved Yahuah's way. Cain killed him, was sent away, and started his own religion, one that is the root of all false religions and beliefs throughout history.[6]

It says of Adam's third son, Seth, that he was fathered in his likeness and image (Gen. 5:3).[7] This is in contrast to Adam himself who was created in the likeness of Elohim (Gen 1:27).

From the above we can see that Yahushua *had* to be born of a virgin—he *had* to be born with the same innocence (and the ability to sin and lose that innocence) that Adam was created with. Praise Yah, he always chose to obey his Father. But this does not make him more than human. Rather, it makes him a human who was extraordinary because (and only because) his Father could live and do things through him

---

5 Flesh in Greek is *sarx*. *Sarx* also refers to the physical body.

6 All false religions, including belief in a god-man and the trinity, can be traced back to him, but that subject is not part of this book.

7 This would apply to Cain and Abel as well.

without any hindrance. That's why he could say, *"If you have seen me, you have seen the Father"* (Jn 14:9).

Therefore, he was *"a lamb without blemish or defect"* (1Pe 1:19). *"He committed no sin, and no deceit was found in his mouth"* (1Pe 2:22). *"In him is no sin"* (1Jn 3:5). *"He was tempted in everything like us, without sin"* (Heb 4:15). Because of this, *"Elohim made him who knew no sin to be sin (or, a sin offering) for us that we might be made the righteousness of Elohim in him"* (2Cor 5:21).

According to Romans 5:12 and 19, *"Sin entered the world through one man, and through sin death. ... For just as through the disobedience of the one man the many were made sinners, so also through the obedience of the one the many will be made righteous."*

Yahushua came from heaven in two ways. The first is by the virgin birth. Yahuah created the seed to fertilize the egg in Miryam (Mary). This way he was not born with an inherited weakness toward sin and was like the first Adam before he sinned, having perfect fellowship with Yahuah and not needing a conscience, the knowledge of good and evil. All his life he always obeyed what his Father told him, either to do or not to do. He had a will of his own like the rest of us, but if what he wanted to do was different from what his Father wanted, he wouldn't know it unless his Father told him, just as it was with Adam and Eve.

Note: The virgin birth did not give him an advantage making it easier for him not to sin and making him more than a human only. He had greater ability, but his testing was that much greater. We are all tested to the limit of our ability. That includes him.

In Scripture we see an example of Yahushua not having a conscience. When he was twelve years old at the temple he stayed behind when his parents and the others with them left (Lk 2:41-51). He stayed doing what he wanted to do because no one, and no inward pricking of conscience, said otherwise.

The other way Yahushua was from heaven is by living his life in heaven; that is, in the will of his Father. Everything he did was from heaven. When our lives are in him, then we also are from heaven. **To be from heaven is figurative language; it is not literal.**

Elohim raised us up with Messiah and seated us with him in the heavenly realms in Messiah Yahushua. (Eph 2:6)

As many as are led by the spirit of Elohim, these are sons of Elohim. (Ro 8:14)

Except for the passage in 1 Corinthians quoted earlier, all other references to Yahushua coming from heaven are in the Gospel of John. **Keep in mind that to come from heaven is figurative and means to come from the authority of heaven, that is, Elohim.**

No one has ever gone into heaven except the one who came from heaven — the Son of Man. (Jn 3:13, NIV)

To go into heaven is figurative and means to get authority from Elohim.

"The one who comes from above is above all; the one who is from the earth belongs to the earth, and speaks as one from the earth. The one who comes from heaven is above all." (Jn 3:31, NIV)

We were created to be from heaven. To belong to the world is figurative of belonging to the ways of sinful man.

"I came from the Father and entered the world; now I am leaving the world and going back to the Father." (Jn 16:28, NIV)

This also is figurative. He came from the authority of the Father and entered the culture of sinful man. The context of this saying is the Last Supper in which Yahushua is giving his disciples instructions before he dies and is raised from death. It must not be taken literally, nor did his disciples understand it to be literal. This kind of figurative language was common in their language and culture.

The other references in John are in chapter 6 in which Yahushua is the bread from heaven and the whole analogy is figurative. Yahuah is spirit and is everywhere. To come from heaven is to come from Elohim's authority.

The reason became flesh.

> And the Word became flesh and lived among us, and we have seen his glory, the glory as of a father's only son, full of grace and truth. (Jn 1:14, NRS)

> That which was from the beginning, which we have heard, which we have seen with our eyes, which we have looked at and our hands have touched— this we proclaim concerning the Word of life. The life appeared; we have seen it and testify to it, and we proclaim to you the eternal life, which was with the Father and has appeared to us. (1Jn 1:1-2, NIV)

When did the reason for creation become created existence? "Become flesh" means you can see it and touch it and experience it. The reason was not seen until it was manifested in Yahushua's ministry, culminating in his death for our sins, resurrection from the grave, and ascension to heaven. This is the true "incarnation," not a non-existent second person of a non-existent one-deity-essence[8] becoming a god-man.

Conclusion

It was in the ministry of Yahushua that the reason for creation became flesh. His was a life fully devoted to the Father. Yahushua said:

> "I am the way, and the truth, and the life. No one comes to the Father except through me." (Jn 14:6, NAS)

---

8 In Trinitarianism the "one God" that is made up of three distinct, individual Persons is an essence, just as humans make up the essence of humanity. The difference is that each of the three is ALL of the essence while being separate Persons, whereas each human is his own humanity.

His life is the way we were created to live, the truth about the whole purpose of life and the nature of the Father, and the life abundant with the Father living in us and we in him.[9] Because of this, he is the mediator, the means, whereby our sins can be forgiven and we can have fellowship with our creator Father for eternity. That is why:

> "Salvation is found in no one else, for there is no other name under heaven given to men by which we must be saved." (Ac 4:12, NIV)

---

9 This means living in the Father's will.

CHAPTER THREE

The Man Prophesied

⎯⎯⎯ ⠀⠀⠀ ⎯⎯⎯

Moses said, "Yahuah your Elohim will raise up for you a prophet like
me from among your own brothers." (Dt 18:15)

T HE PURPOSE OF THIS CHAPTER IS TO show that the prophecies of the coming Messiah are about a man, a human only, not a
god-man. Dual-naturists (this includes both Trinitarians and Oneness[1])
believe Jesus is fully human, but the kind of human they believe he is is
not human like all other humans are human, because they believe he is
also fully deity. Therefore, even though they *say* they believe in the true
humanity of Yahushua, in reality they don't.

I have asked non-clergy dual-naturist church people (those who are
not trained in the double-talk of clergy), "Is Jesus human like all other
humans are human?" The answer has always been the same: "No. He is
not human like we are because he is also God." To them the 100% God
part nullifies the 100% human part. They believe everything he did was
because he was God. Even the humanity that died was God.

I have also asked these people, "Is it possible to overcome all sin in
our lives?" The answer: "No. Because we are human we cannot overcome
sin. The only reason Jesus never sinned is because he is God, and God
can't sin."

What a lie! What deception! The devil doesn't want us to know that
we humans *can* overcome all sin, and that's because Yahushua, a 100%

---

1 See Supplement on Oneness.

true human only, overcame sin. Yahushua died for us not only that our sins be forgiven and we be reconciled to the Father, but that we also can live *without* sin. With him in us so that we are living in the spirit, we not only can live without sin, but we can do the mighty works that he did, that the apostles did, and that he commanded us to do.

The doctrine of eternal security—once saved, always saved—is part of this deception. This false teaching says: *"All you have to do to have your sins forgiven and go to heaven is to receive Jesus into your heart and confess him as Lord. Once you do that, all your past sins and future sins are forgiven. Once you are saved you can never lose your salvation no matter how much you sin or how wicked you are. The blood of Jesus Christ covers it all. Hallelujah."*

This belief is from the devil, and it will take you to hell. How you start the race is important, but how you finish it determines your salvation. Salvation is a day-to-day commitment of endurance to overcome sin and please the Father because of love for him and what his nature is. *"He who endures to the end will be saved"* (Mt 10:22, NKJ).

> If anyone would come after me, he must deny himself and take up his cross **daily** and follow me. For whoever wants to save his life will lose it, but whoever loses his life for me will save it. (Lk 9:23-24, NIV)

> I discipline my body and bring *it* into subjection, lest, when I have preached to others, I myself should become disqualified. (1Cor 9:27, NKJ)

I trust that this information helps you realize how important to salvation is the truth that Yahushua is a human only, for in this truth you realize that you are able to overcome all sin in your life. And with the truth of the humanity only of Yahushua is the truth that Elohim is an absolute one only.

NOTE: The foundation lie of the Trinity is belief in the dual nature of Christ, a lie forced on the church by imperial decree at the Council of Nicea in 325 C.E. When this belief is shown to be false, then the doctrine of the Trinity falls. Without the Second Person there is no Trinity, and the holy spirit is seen for what it is, that it is the holy Father just as your spirit is you.

The prophecy of Moses in Deuteronomy 18:15, quoted at the beginning of this chapter, said that the coming Messiah was a man like himself, and Moses was a human only, not a god-man.

Many prophecies in the Old Testament show that the promised Messiah would be a human. He would be born of a woman, (Gen 3:15; Gal 4:4), he would come from the tribe of Judah, (Gen 49:10; Heb 7:14), and he would come from king David of that tribe, (2Sa 7:12-13; Is 9:7; Lk 1:32-33; Ro 1:3).

Two other prophecies provide additional information, information which requires some examination because it is used by dual-naturists to support their belief. During this examination, we will follow the rules of interpretation that Scripture cannot contradict itself and that seeming contradictions must be clarified by the clear Scriptures that say Messiah is a man. Words must mean what they mean, so man means man only.

The first of the two prophecies was discussed briefly in the Introduction.

The pregnant virgin will give birth to a son,[2] and will call him Immanuel. (Is 7:14)

Below is the other prophecy that needs examination.

For a child will be born to us, a son will be given to us; And the government will rest on His shoulders; And His name will be called Wonderful Counselor, Mighty God, Eternal Father, Prince of Peace. (Is 9:6, NAS)

Trinitarians believe that this prophecy shows the deity of Messiah, for he is called "Mighty God." Wait! Big problem. What about "Wonderful Counselor" and "Eternal Father." These are the Third and First Persons of the Trinity? And they are in the wrong order. So is this saying that the Messiah is all three Persons of the Trinity? This is madness.

---

2 Can God be born and be a child?

The Hebrew for "Mighty God" is *el gibbor*. It can mean strong magistrate.

Note: the verse does not say he *is* these things, but that his *name* will be *called* these things; that is, his *nature* is called these things. What is his name? It is Yahushua. What does Yahushua mean? It means "Yahuah salvation," or "Yahuah the savior" or "Yahuah is salvation."

And what does Yahuah mean? It is the personal name of Elohim, our creator and Father, and means "He is" or "the self-existing one." Yahushua has the name of the Father in his name. All that the Father is, his nature, is in Yahushua the man (Col 2:9). This human is the image of the invisible Elohim (Col 1:15). He is his exact representation (Heb 1:3). That is what these verses are saying. And this is what we are created to be. Yahushua is our pattern—the way, the truth and the life—showing us that through him we can be that way. When the dark cloud of dual-naturist thinking is gone, and when Scripture is used to interpret Scripture, and when words mean what they mean, then truth can be seen.

This prophecy is also seen in the command to immerse into the name (nature) of the Father, and of the son, and of the spirit of set-apartness (Mt 28:19). This also was discussed in the Introduction.

Conclusion

The prophecies regarding Messiah are about a man, a human only, but what a most wonderful man he is. He is our pattern, our big brother. Let us believe in him for what Scripture says he is, not for what pagan, church, orthodox tradition says he is.

CHAPTER FOUR

The Man "Worshiped"

—⊸⊶⊷⊶⊷⊷—

They saw the child with Mary his mother; and they knelt down and paid
him homage. (Mt 2:11, NRS)

"pay homage" Gk *proskunéō.* In the NT, generally, to do reverence or homage to someone, usually by kneeling or prostrating oneself before him. In the Septuagint it means to bow down, to prostrate
oneself in reverence, homage (Gen 19:1; 48:12).[1]

Hb *shāchāh*: A verb meaning to bow down, to prostrate oneself,
to crouch, to fall down, to humbly beseech, to do reverence, to worship. The primary meaning of the word is to bow down. This verb is
used to indicate bowing before a monarch or a superior and paying
homage to him or her (Gen 43:28).[2]

Worship 1. a. The reverent love and devotion accorded a deity,
an idol, or a sacred object.[3]

MOST ENGLISH TRANSLATIONS USE THE WORD "WORSHIP"
for both the Greek and Hebrew words when they think the one
being reverenced is deity. But it is a general word that is applied also

---

1 Strong's # NT4352. Word Study Dictionary of the New Testament.

2 Strong's # OT7342. Word Study Dictionary of the Old Testament.

3 The American Heritage Dictionary.

to humans. So whenever you see the word "worship" in various English translations of Scripture, it is important to realize that it is *commentary* to show deity; it is *not translation*. It is the *object* of *proskuneō* or *shāchāh* that shows whether it is worship of deity, not the word itself.

Very few Bible readers, including pastors, know Greek or Hebrew, so they assume that what they see is correct. One of the arguments that Trinitarian teachers use to support their belief that Yahushua is deity is the word "worship." In the minds of Trinitarians, Yahushua *is* deity, so they use "worship." But, as we have seen, he is a man, a human only, a most incredible man, but not deity. It would be better if the word "worship" were never used in Scripture translations and let the reader decide from the context what is happening. Also, the word "worship" hides the physical act being done even if it is for deity.

When the Magi came to pay homage to the child, they were coming because of a sign that the prophecy of the coming king of the Jews was fulfilled. They were coming to show honor to a human child, not to worship a god.

Proskuneō is used 65 times in 54 verses. In the NIV it is used 17 times to refer to Yahushua. Mostly it is translated as "worship." Other NIV translations of this same word are "knelt before him" (three times), "kneeling down" (one time), "fall on his knees" (one time), "paid homage" (one time). It is interesting to note that the passages which refer to kneeling have to do with people seeking help for healing, and the passage for paying homage is by the soldiers when they beat him before having him executed (Mk 15:1). But it's the same Greek word. The word is also used for general worship, for worshiping Satan, demons and the antichrist beast, and in a parable of a servant to his master (Mt 18:26).

Cornelius *"fell at his feet in reverence"* to Peter, and John did it to two angels in his vision of the last days. All rejected these acts, Peter on the basis of being a man, and the angels on the basis of being fellow servants (Ac 10:25; Rev 19:10; 22:8).

One other usage is the message to the assembly in Philadelphia.

> "I will make those who are of the synagogue of Satan, who claim to be Jews though they are not, but are liars— I will make them come and **fall down** at your feet and acknowledge that I have loved you. (Rev 3:9, NIV)

Conclusion

As we have seen, the word "worship" is misleading when used in Scripture, for it doesn't show the physical act being done. We see an example of the physical act in Muslim worship. They kneel and touch their foreheads to the ground. But what about us in our Western and Christian culture of today? We speak of a whole service being a "worship service," and we also speak of the singing time as "worship."

I urge you therefore, brethren, by the mercies of God, to present your bodies a living and holy sacrifice, acceptable to God, *which is* your spiritual **service of worship**. (Ro 12:1, NAS)

The phrase "service of worship" is from the Greek word *latreia.*

1) service rendered for hire 1a) any service or ministration: the service of God 2) the service and worship of God according to the requirements of the Levitical law 3) to perform sacred services.[4]

This Greek word is similar to the Hebrew word *'avad.* It is a verb meaning "to work, to serve."[5] The most common usage is serving a person of higher position. But when the context is doing a religious service to Yahuah, such as in the tabernacle or temple, it is translated as "serve" or "worship," depending on the Scripture version.

With this Scripture meaning in mind, we "worship" either Yahushua or his Father Yahuah when we serve them, as it says in Romans 12:1 quoted above.

We will look at "worship" again in the dialogue of Yahushua with Satan in "Chapter 7 The Man Tempted." The purpose of this chapter is to show that the use of the word "worship" for Yahushua is misleading and it cannot be used to show deity.

---

4 Strong's NT2999 in BibleWorks database.

5 Strong's OT5647 in BibleWorks database.

CHAPTER FIVE

The Man Immersed

———⊗⊗⊗———

"I [John] baptize you with water for repentance. But after me will come one who is more powerful than I, whose sandals I am not fit to carry. He will baptize you with the Holy Spirit and with fire." (Mt 3:11, NIV)

As Yahushua was coming up out of the water, he saw heaven being torn open and the spirit descending on him like a dove. And a voice came from heaven: "You are my son, whom I love; with you I am well pleased." (Mk 1:10-11)

JOHN'S IMMERSION[1] WAS FOR REPENTANCE. WHY THEN did Yahushua, who was sinless, come to him to be immersed? When John didn't want to do it his answer to John was:

"Let it be so now; it is **proper for us** to do this **to fulfill all righteousness**." (Mt 3:15, NIV, emphasis added)

We will analyze this verse to see what Yahushua was saying. We note that this event involved fulfilling all righteousness, and the fulfilling of it involved both John and Yahushua. John's message, symbolized in the act of immersion in water, was for repentance: *"Repent, for the kingdom of heaven is at hand"* (Mt 3:2). This also was the message of Yahushua when

---

1 The Greek word *baptidzo*, from which we get the word "baptism," means immersion.

33

he began his ministry (Mt 4:17). So repentance (turning away from sin) was involved even though Yahushua didn't need to repent. John announced of him, *"Look, the lamb of Elohim who takes away the sin of the world!"* (Jn 1:29).

Adam Clarke's Commentary on John 1:29 has an excellent article.

> This was said in allusion to what was spoken in Isa 53:7. Jesus was the true Lamb or Sacrifice required and appointed by God, of which those offered daily in the tabernacle and temple, Ex 29:38-39, and especially the paschal [Passover] lamb, were only the types and representatives. See Ex 12:4-5; 1 Cor 5:7. The continual morning and evening sacrifice of a lamb, under the Jewish law, was intended to point out the continual efficacy of the blood of atonement: for even at the throne of God Jesus Christ is ever represented as a lamb newly slain, Rev 5:6. But John, pointing to Christ, calls him emphatically, the Lamb of God:-all the lambs which had been hitherto offered had been furnished by men: this was provided by GOD, as the only sufficient and available sacrifice for the sin of the world. In three essential respects, this lamb differed from those by which it was represented.
>
> 1. It was the Lamb of God; the most excellent, and the most available.
>
> 2. It made an atonement for sin: it carried sin away in reality, the others only representatively.
>
> 3. It carried away the sin of the WORLD, whereas the other was offered only on behalf of the Jewish people.[2]

We need also to look at water immersion among believers. In the book of Acts we see that when believers were immersed it was in the name of Yahushua Messiah and for the forgiveness of sins (Ac 2:38). In this immersion we identify with him by being buried with him through

---

2 Adam Clarke's Commentary in BibleSoft.

immersion into his death. It represents our old man being impaled with him so that the body of sin might be made powerless and we no longer serve sin and become alive in Messiah (Ro 6:3-11). Also in this identification, we clothe ourselves with him so that his righteousness covers our sin and people see his nature in us (Gal 3:27).

In all of this, our immersion is symbolic of identification with the one in whose name we are immersed. For believers, that name is Yahushua Messiah. When we put our faith in him through obedience, as Abraham did by offering his son Isaac, then he becomes our righteousness (1Cor 1:30; Ro 4:9).

Yahushua (a most extraordinary man but a man only) is the last Adam (1Cor 15:45). Even as the first Adam represents mankind, so does this last Adam. Everything he did was on behalf of mankind. This includes his immersion by John. Immersion for us, as we have seen, represents death and resurrection (going under water in burial and coming up in new life). It is the same for him. In three and a half short years he would die and be buried and three days later rise from the grave. Regarding his death, Yahushua told James and John they would drink the cup he drinks and be immersed in the immersion in which he is immersed (Mk 10:39). This immersion refers to dying to self daily (Lk 9:23).

Besides identification there are other reasons for his immersion—*"It is proper for us."* In this act they were validating each other's ministry, that each was indeed from Elohim, that what they did was by the authority of Elohim.

Again, John was the forerunner of the Messiah, preparing the way for him, carrying the message: *"The kingdom of heaven is near."* Messiah was now here, so he handed the message over to him to complete it. *"He must increase, but I must decrease"* (Jn 3:30).

Another reason for immersion is that Yahushua was being anointed to begin his ministry. He was about 30 years old, and that is the age in which priests were anointed to begin their ministry. Their priesthood was after the order of Aaron, his after the order of Melchizedek (Gen 14:18; Heb 5:6; 7:11).

A final reason for his immersion, a false one, is that whenever Trinitarians see a verse that has "THE THREE" in it, they jump on it as proof (or evidence) that the one God is made up of three Persons.[3] This is one of such passages. They allege that this event is evidence of the Trinity—God the Father (the voice), God the Son (the man), and God the Holy Spirit (the dove), three-in-one and one-in-three, the blessed Trinity. Count them: one, two, three.

A look at this event reveals no such thing, nothing even remotely coming close, rather the opposite. If the Scriptures *said* in clear verses that God is a trinity of three equal Persons, each the totality of God-essence yet each separate and distinct from the other (a logical impossibility), and that the Son is infinite deity while at the same time being finite man (another logical impossibility) then this event could be interpreted by those clear verses. But they don't.

Rather, the Scriptures say Elohim is one, the Father, that his spirit is himself (just as your spirit is yourself), and his son is a man. So what happened? All agree that Yahushua is a man. All agree that the Father caused sound waves of speaking (a created event) that people could hear. And all agree that the dove (a created bird) is symbolic of the spirit. But does this make a trinity of three Persons? It is a stretch of the imagination and logic that can only come from a preconceived belief, not from clear Scripture. Remember, "words must mean what they mean" and "clear verses must be used to interpret unclear ones." This verse is clear, and there is nothing of a trinity of Persons in it.

The next event in the life of Yahushua is his temptation in the wilderness. But before we go there we need to look at another character in the garden of Eden. He is the adversary, Satan. There is a parallel between what happened in that garden and what happened in the wilderness.

3　An example among many is: http://www.gotquestions.org/Jesus-baptized.html

CHAPTER SIX

The Adversary

—⚬⚬⚬—

> When the woman saw that the fruit of the tree was good for food and pleasing to the eye, and also desirable for gaining wisdom, she took some and ate it. ... The woman said [to Yahuah Elohim], "The serpent deceived me, and I ate." (Gen 3:6,13, NIV)

THE SERPENT, OF COURSE, REFERS TO SATAN, a Hebrew word meaning "adversary." He is involved throughout the history of mankind and is seen throughout Scripture. He is a real spirit being, a being of great power. We will not go into detail regarding the many things the Scriptures say about him. Rather, our concern in this chapter is where he came from and how he operates.

In Isaiah 14:12-15 and Ezekiel 28:11-9 we see two descriptions of him. These words, in poetry form, are addressed to the kings of Babylon and Tyre, but they refer to Satan, for his spirit is in them, moving them to do what they do. In these poems we see an exalted angelic being, the highest of the created angels, who, because of pride, wanted to become like the Most High and sit on his throne. As a result he was thrown out of heaven along with many angels who sided with him in his rebellion. Satan became the devil and the other rebels became demons.

Angels are ministering spirits sent to serve those who will inherit salvation (Heb 1:14). They were created to be our servants, not only to help us come into the kingdom, but to serve us (those of us who come into the kingdom) for eternity. In fact, we will be their judges (1Cor 6:3).

It is easy to connect this fact with the reaction among the angels when they learned that we weak humans will be higher than they and have a much closer relationship with the Almighty than they. Only we humans will make up the bride of Yahuah Elohim and his son Yahushua, not they. This was a test for them, even as the tree of the knowledge of good and evil was a test for Adam and Eve.

Satan, in his pride, along with many other angels, didn't like the idea. They didn't want to be servants. They wanted to rule. So they were kicked out and became the enemies of man. They are beings of free will as we humans are. They were in the very presence of their creator, experiencing all his love directly. And they rejected it. By so doing they became spirits of hatred, cruelty and darkness—all that is opposite of the nature of Yahuah.

A question asked by many is why did God create angels knowing that one would become Satan and many become demons? The answer is the same as to why he created man knowing they would sin and the majority go to hell. The few who make it to become his darling bride, those who will be one with him to share his nature with one another for eternity, are worth the many who don't (Mt 7:13-14). Regarding angels becoming the devil and demons, despite their hatred of their creator and mankind, Yahuah is using them on behalf of man. Man needs testing, and all things work together for good to those who love him and are called according to his purpose (Ro 8:28). Satan and his demons exist because in our Father's wisdom he uses them for our good.

Our concern here is their power to seduce into disobeying Yahuah. That's what Satan did to Eve. Temptation comes in three ways.

> For all that is in the world, (1) the lust of the flesh and (2) the lust of the eyes and (3) the boastful pride of life, is not from the Father, but is from the world. (1 Jn 2:16, NAS, numbering added)

Notice the comparison with Eve's temptation.

> When the woman saw that the fruit of the tree was (1) good for food and (2) pleasing to the eye, and also (3) desirable for gaining wisdom, she took some and ate it. (Gen 3:6, numbering added)

Back to 1 John 2:16. "Flesh" refers to our animal appetites. Our bodies have a "mind." It "talks" to us regarding hunger, thirst, sleep, comfort seeking and pain avoidance, and sex. These are "drives" the creator created in us. It is what all animals have. But Elohim made rules regarding how to handle these drives, and our souls decide to obey or disobey them. Our bodies don't make decisions; our souls do. That's where our free will resides.

Our souls also have desires. The soul "talks" to us regarding intangible things, such as beauty, companionship, wanting or not wanting children, possession of things, submission and control, obedience and disobedience, humility and pride, love and hate, all the variety of emotions—the list is long.

Again, our spirits have desires. It "talks" to us regarding things in the spirit realm. Through this medium Elohim is drawing our souls to the light of his nature of selfless love for him to be our Father, and the devil is drawing our souls to the darkness of his nature of selfishness for him to be our father. Our souls—our free wills—decide which to yield to. There is no middle ground: in any event either Yahuah is our Father or the devil is. Yahushua said to the Jews who didn't believe in him but claimed that Elohim was their father:

> "You belong to your father, the devil, and you want to carry out your father's desire. He was a murderer from the beginning, not holding to the truth, for there is no truth in him. When he lies, he speaks his native language, for he is a liar and the father of lies." (Jn 8:44, NIV)

What happened in "the forbidden fruit" incident? Why did Adam and Eve disobey Yahuah's command? Paul's first letter to Timothy has an interesting comment on what happened.

> Adam was not the one deceived; it was the woman who was deceived and became a sinner. (1Ti 2:14, NIV)

When we compare it with the Genesis account, this is a very strange statement. To help understand it we need to look to typology, for the whole of creation is typological of things spiritual.

Typology

Typology is the study of types. A type is a physical person, thing or event that points to something spiritual. The thing that it points to is called the antitype. For example, Adam is a type of Messiah because many things about him point to the last Adam, Messiah Yahushua. In this case, Messiah is an antitype of Adam. Women are a type of the assembly: good women are a type of the bride of Messiah, and bad women are a type of the wicked assembly. The assembly, of course, is made up of both men and women. Many things that women do are types of what the assembly does, such as caring for children and those who are ill.

Women are more emotional than men. They tend to follow their emotions when making decisions more so than men do. In contrast, men depend more on reason and less on emotion. (These are general statements.) This is why Elohim created men to lead and women to help them and support them. Eve was created as a helper for Adam. This has nothing to do with intellectual ability, for many women are smarter than men, and wives than their husbands. It has to do with created position.

> And I wish you to know that the head of every man is the Messiah, and the head of woman is the man, and the head of Messiah is the Elohim. (1Cor 11:3) [1]

Just as every good woman mentioned in Scripture is a type of the bride of Messiah, so every good man mentioned in Scripture is a type of Messiah. An excellent example of this is Joseph. There are more things mentioned about him that are types of Messiah than any other man.

Adam and Eve both sinned, and together they brought sin into the world. Eve, because she was deceived, did not think she was disobeying Yahuah. Adam, because he was not deceived, knew that he was

---

1 See also Eph 5:22-24.

disobeying. He loved her and so knowingly joined her in death. It was an immediate spiritual death, but that day (a day is as a thousand years, 2Pe 3:8) they both died physically. The antitype of this is Yahushua dying for us because of his love for us. Also in the account is Eve being taken from Adam's side.[2] The antitype is the bride coming from Messiah's side which was pierced.

With this typology in mind, in 1 Timothy 2:14 Adam, the one not deceived, is a type of Messiah. And the woman, the one deceived and who became a sinner, is a type of all mankind.[3]

Regarding types, be aware that types are only spiritual illustrations that add understanding to their antitypes; for example, Joseph's experiences add understanding to Messiah. The OT was written to shed light on NT truths (1Cor 10:11). Doctrine should never be based on types, and types fit where they fit. That is, if something in the life of an Old Testament character doesn't fit with the antitype, even though other things do, then that thing is not a type. For example, Adam's love for his wife and giving up his life to be with her is a type of Messiah's love for us and giving up his life for us, but his disobedience is not a type of Messiah.

Deception

Deception is believing something is true that is not true; all deception comes from the devil and his demons; and we are deceived because something in us wants to be deceived.[4]

When Lucifer and his followers rebelled against all that is true and good and beautiful, they did so with full knowledge of the consequences. They would rather be evil beings of hate and wickedness and go to eternal torment in hell than submit to their creator. During the Millennium when Messiah rules on earth there will be no deception, because the devil and his demons will be in the Abyss during that time (Rev 20:1-3). Anyone sinning during that time will do so with the full knowledge of

---

2 The Hebrew can mean rib, but mostly it refers to the side.

3 Other explanations have been given, but this is the way it seems to me.

4 See 1Ki 19:22-23; 2Th 2:9-12.

their rebellion against the Almighty. All false religion and doctrines are the result of deception.

Deception comes from yielding to seduction.[5] Something comes upon you that feels good. Mostly we are not aware of the pull of the demon because we are so used to yielding that it seems natural. But there is a spiritual pull, and it comes from a demon. I wish to relate such a pull that opened my eyes.

I was enjoying a walk in Twin Falls State Park near North Bend, Washington, an area lived in by the Snoqualmie Tribe for over a century.[6] As I neared the Falls I came around a bend in the trail and there before me, across the gorge, was the white, smooth surface of a large granite rock. The sun was shining full on it. The scene was beautiful. I didn't hear words in my natural ears, but I did in my spirit: "Worship me." I felt the awe and the pull to bow to it and to acknowledge it as a god. The Snoqualmie people, as with all Native American tribes, are nature worshipers. They especially worship any unusual natural formation because they can "feel" the demon in it, and it feels good and right. That demon was still there.

We don't know what pull Eve felt when the serpent tempted her, but it felt good and right to body, soul and spirit. She opened to that appeal of feeling, she wanted it, and was deceived.

With this as a background we turn to Messiah's temptation.

---

5 E.g.; The woman Folly in Proverbs 7.

6 1844. www.goia.wa.gov/tribal-information/Tribes/snoqualmie.htm

CHAPTER SEVEN

The Man Tempted

———⚬⚬⚬———

Jesus, full of the Holy Spirit, returned from the Jordan and was led by the Spirit in the desert, where for forty days he was tempted by the devil. He ate nothing during those days, and at the end of them he was hungry. (Lk 4:1-2, NIV)

We have one who has been **tempted in every way, just as we are—** yet was without sin. (Heb 4:15)

"All these things I will give you, if you **fall down** and **prostrate yourself to show homage to** me." Yahushua said to him, "Away from me, Satan! For it is written: **'Prostrate yourself to show homage to** Yahuah your Elohim, and **serve** him only.'" (Mt 4:9-10)

"**Fear** Yahuah your Elohim and **serve** him. (Dt 6:13)

TWO TOPICS ARE COVERED IN THIS CHAPTER—WORSHIP and temptation. Because we previously looked at worship we will continue with it here and then get to the temptation part. What follows may be a bit technical for some, but I like to dig deep to get the most out of a verse, and I find the findings are worth it.

"Worship"

The quote mentioned earlier from Matthew 4:9-10 is a literal translation. Notice I avoided using the word "worship." Two Greek words are translated as worship. The most common is *proskunéo*: "to bow or prostrate oneself in homage to." The other is *latreúo*: "to serve as a hired servant as opposed to a slave."[1] Because it corresponds to what the priests did as servants of the temple, some translations translate it as "worship." But this mix misses the meanings of the originals.

Yahushua quoted from Deuteronomy 6:13 to reject Satan's temptation. In this verse it is interesting to note the difference between what the Hebrew verse says and what the Greek says. The Hebrew uses "fear" (*yārē*) instead of "prostrate" (*shāchāh*). Yahushua, of course, would have quoted the Hebrew in Hebrew, not in Greek. But the Greek gives an added dimension.

"Fear" when directed to Yahuah means "reverential fear." You hold him in awe, not wanting to do anything to displease him, but rather to love him for the greatness that he is. For this reason some translators translate it as "worship." But again, using the word "worship" misses what is really meant.

The three temptations

First we should note that *"Elohim cannot be tempted by evil"* (Jam 1:13). Dual-naturists—those who believe Yahushua is a god-man, 100% deity and 100% humanity—say that as deity he could not be tempted, but as humanity he could. They also say that although he was human, his humanity is different from all other humans. Some say the temptations weren't real.[2] But Scripture says he was tempted in every way the same as we are (Jam 1:13). And, as we have seen, Scripture says he was a man, and man doesn't mean god-man.

---

1 Strong's # 3000, Word Study Dictionary of the New Testament.

2 Those wanting documentation can do a web search on the internet.

The temptations were real, and they were powerful and seductive. It wasn't some low-level demon coming to him; it was the top one, the devil himself. And it wasn't just words he was hearing; he was feeling a spiritual drug-like seduction, like the woman Folly described in Proverbs 7.

He was tested to his limit, but not beyond his limit. Elohim will not allow anyone to be tempted beyond his ability to resist (1Cor 10:13). And when we resist, the devil must flee (Jam 4:7). Nevertheless, it was a struggle. His limit was very high, for when he left the Jordan to go into the desert he was *"full of the spirit of set-apartness"* (Lk 4:1).

We should note that he didn't just casually decide, "I think I will go out into the desert for awhile and do some fasting." No. It wasn't his decision to go. The spirit "drove" him out (Mk 1:12). It was a strong pressure in his spirit: "I *have* to go out." This came right after his immersion by John in which he heard his Father say, *"You are **the** son of me, **the** beloved one. In you I am well pleased"* (Lk 3:22).[3] He was about to begin his ministry as Messiah and he needed to be tested to see if he was ready for the job. And, of course, there would be testing throughout his ministry, culminating in the Garden of Gethsemane in which the agony was so strong that his sweat was like drops of blood falling to the ground: *"Not my will, but yours be done"* (Lk 22:44, 42).

The three temptations that Yahushua faced (Mt 4:1-11) are parallel with the three that Eve faced: body, soul and spirit. The first was his body: *"If you are son of the Elohim, tell these stones to become bread"* (Mt 4:3).[4] After 40 days of no food he was very hungry. Some of the stones would resemble buns, the kind of bread commonly eaten, and Satan would have caused Yahushua to smell fresh baked bread hot from the oven.[5]

Commentaries differ on some points as to what this temptation was. Note that Satan in the temptation didn't use the title "**the** son of Elohim."[6] Satan was taunting Yahushua to prove to him (Satan) that he was the Messiah, and perhaps also to prove it to himself. Anyway,

3 The article "the" in the Greek shows emphasis.

4 "Son" (*huios*) has no article. "Elohim" (*theos*) does have.

5 Satan and demons have ability to make us sense things that aren't there.

6 The Greek is not consistent regarding an article with "son." It depends on the context and the emphasis desired.

besides the wonderful aroma, Satan was giving him feelings of low self esteem and insecurity: "I need to prove to Satan that I really am son of Elohim, and I can do it by turning these stones into bread. And I really am hungry, very hungry." Yahushua rebuffed the temptation by quoting Deuteronomy 8:3: *"Man shall not live by bread alone"* (Lk 4:4).[7]

Could Yahushua have turned the stones into bread? Trinitarians say he could, because he is God as well as man. This brings up the whole issue of miracles. Dual-naturists say the miracles that Yahushua did prove he is deity, for man can't do miracles. If that is so, then Peter and Paul and all those in the Old Testament who did miracles are deity also. When Paul with Barnabas healed a cripple in Lystra the people shouted, *"The gods* (Gk theoi) *have come down to us in human form."* They called Barnabas Zeus and Paul Hermes and wanted to sacrifice to them (Ac 14:8ff).

It is this pagan deception that led to the doctrine of the dual nature of Christ, and then to the doctrine of the Trinity. These are strong words, but they need to be said. Belief in the dual nature of Christ and in the Trinity is a deception no different from the deception in the garden of Eden. They come from Satan and they have been strongholds in the church ever since the Council of Nicea in C.E. 325. They are part of Babylon that the church is called to come out of so as not to share in Babylon's judgment (Jer 51:45; Rev 18:4).

Every false doctrine (of which these are two) has demons attached to it to deceive people into believing it. The more irrational and "against reason" the doctrine is,[8] the higher in authority the demon is. The ones over these doctrines are arch-demons. The pull to believe them is very strong, like an addiction. Many who come out of them experience "withdrawal symptoms." They now know the truth, but they feel demonic lying emotions that the truth is false. I speak from the testimonies of others and also from my own experience. The less trained in or exposed to the doctrine, the easier it is to believe the truth. The converse is also true, the more trained in or exposed to the doctrine, the harder it is to leave the lie.

---

7 Mt 4:4 adds *"but by every word coming out of the mouth of God."*

8 Trinitarians justify their irrational doctrine by saying it is a reason higher than reason.

I have been free from that demonic pull for over 20 years, but when I started writing this book I could feel it again, and I could feel Yahuah's hatred of that doctrine for calling him a liar that he is not one but three-in-one and that his son is not a human but a god-man.

Know this: Man cannot do any miracles by themselves, but Elohim in man has done them,[9] can do them, and does do them. Because of his relationship with the Father, Yahushua could have turned the stones into bread. Would it have been a sin if he did? By itself, turning stones to bread wouldn't be sin unless his Father told him not to. Later in his ministry it wasn't a sin to turn water into wine nor was it sin to walk on water and calm the storm. In the case of the stones, however, it was a temptation that came from the prince of darkness. Yahushua would not use darkness to promote his ministry that he is the Messiah, the son of Elohim. *"Do not do evil that good may come"* (Ro 3:8). Also he would only say what he heard the Father say and only do what he saw him do. He was not operating from his own natural decisions; he was walking in the spirit (Jn 10:37-38).

Satan's next temptation (Mt 4:5-7) was directed at Yahushua's soul. By means of a vision he took Yahushua to Jerusalem and had him stand on the highest point of the temple where again he challenged his position as son of Elohim by telling him to jump off so angels could catch him, quoting Psalm 91:11-12. Would they have caught him? Yes they would. Satan was appealing to pride. People would see it happen and he would be lifted up in their eyes as the Messiah.

Yahushua's response was to quote Scripture again. *"You shall not test Yahuah your Elohim"* (Dt 6:16). In this response Yahushua was saying that if he were to jump off the temple peak he would be testing Yahuah as did the children of Israel in the wilderness by complaining of no water and asking, *"Is Yahuah among us or not?"* (Ex 17:7). They were complaining because of unbelief. In that incident Moses struck the rock at Horeb and water came out. Yahuah answered their request despite their unbelief. In effect, Yahushua's reply to Satan was that if he were to obey the temptation it would be because of unbelief in his Father. Yahushua was not going to exalt himself by his own mind or emotions, and certainly not by

---

9 Moses, Elijah and Elisha all did miracles.

the suggestion of the devil. He was trusting Yahuah to exalt him in his own timing and in his own way.

Satan's third temptation was directed at Yahushua's spirit. This also was by means of a vision. This was touched on at the beginning of this chapter, but there is more to discuss.

> The devil led him up to a high place and showed him in an instant all the kingdoms of the world. And he said to him, "I will give you all their authority and splendor, for it has been given to me, and I can give it to anyone I want to. So if you worship me, it will all be yours." (Lk 4: 5-7, NIV)

No physical place is high enough to see around the globe, and physically we can't see kingdoms. What Satan was showing him was the splendor of the world system; that is, the world system of governments and religions and the people involved in them under the leadership of Satan. In other words, he was showing Messiah how wonderful the kingdom of Satan is. Elohim calls this system Babylon.[10]

Before we go further we need to look at Satan's authority on earth and how he got it. 2 Corinthians 4:4 speaks of the god (Gk *theos*) of this age (Gk *iōn*). *Iōn* (from which we get our English word "eon") has to do with an indefinite long period of time, or, as in this verse, a specific long period of time. Satan is the "god" of this *iōn*/age, age referring to when his "godship" began to the time when it will end. It is a specific time period, about 6000 years, starting from the time Adam and Eve sinned to when the Messiah returns to start his rule of 1000 years, called the Millennium.

Satan is also called *"the prince of this world* (kosmos). *"* (Jn 12:31) *Kosmos* means "the order of things." We get several English words from it, such as cosmos, cosmetics and cosmopolitan.

In Scripture *kosmos*/world usually refers to people who live in an ordered society ruled by Satan. When Yahushua said to the Jews, *"You are from below; I am from above. You are of this world; I am not of this world"* (Jn

---

10 I don't know about you, the reader, but to me the world system is horrible and wicked, full of wars, hatred, corruption and every vile thing. *"The heart is deceitful above all things, and desperately wicked: who can know it?"* (Jer 17:9, KJV).

8:23), he was not talking about physical locations of earth versus heaven where Elohim and angels live, but spiritual locations of the kingdom of Satan (darkness) versus the kingdom of heaven (light). We believers are from above as lights in this world. Because we are born from above,[11] we are from above. "Above" is the realm in which the man Yahushua lived. In everything he did he was from above reaching out to those who live "below."

All authority is from the Father. He gives it to whom he will and takes it from whom he will.

> "... the Most High is sovereign over the kingdoms of men and gives them to anyone he wishes ..." (Dan 4:17, NIV)

> There is no authority except that which God has established. The authorities that exist have been established by God. (Ro 13:1, NIV)

It was Elohim who gave Satan authority, a limited authority. It was authority over mankind who submit to him as their god, joining him in his rebellion against Yahuah. But even then it is limited. He has to get permission from Yahuah to do anything. We see this when he requested permission to attack Job (Job 1:8- 2:7). He cannot tempt us beyond our ability to resist (1Cor 10:13). And if we resist him, he must run away from us (Jam 4:7).

Satan was trying to dazzle Yahushua with the beauty of his darkness and corruption, tempting him to acknowledge him as his strong one and in return to serve him as vice-regent to rule the world system. Yahushua replied with Scripture: *"Away from me, Satan! For it is written: 'Worship Yahuah your Elohim, and serve him only'"* (Mt 4:10).

Conclusion

All of these temptations are of a man, a very remarkable man but still a man only, a man as human as you and I are and all the rest of mankind. The only difference is he was born of a virgin (to be like the first

---

11 Jn 3:3. "Born again" also means "born from above."

man before he sinned), and he always obeyed his Father (unlike the first man), and so he was without sin. His being sinless was not because of being deity and not because of being born of a virgin without a predisposition to sin. This gave him no advantage, for his temptations were that much harder. He was tested to his limit just as we are. Remember, Adam and Eve were created perfect without any predisposition to sin, yet still sinned. Rather, Yahushua was sinless because of loving the Father with all his heart, soul, mind and strength and his neighbor as himself, always (Lk 10:27). This we also are commanded to do, and because of him, the price that he paid, we can do it, but only with him in us (Col 1:27).

CHAPTER EIGHT

The Man's Authority

———— ❧ ————

"Men of Israel, listen to this: Jesus of Nazareth was a man accredited by God to you by miracles, wonders and signs, which God did among you through him, as you yourselves know." (Ac 2:22, NIV)

DUAL-NATURISTS SAY THAT THE MIRACLES THAT JESUS did show that he is deity, for only God can do these things. It is true that only Elohim can do miracles, but often he does them through the authority he gives to certain men. Therefore, doing miracles are not the sign of deity, but the sign of authority given by deity.

The Old Testament is full of miracles, either by the direct action of Elohim or through men. A man says, prays or does something, and Yahuah does the miracle. Moses, Elijah and Elisha are examples of humans doing miracles. With his rod Moses parted the Red Sea and got water out of rock (Ex 14:21-31; 17:6). Both Elijah and Elisha each raised a boy from the dead (1Ki 17:17-24; 2Ki 4:32-37). Elisha knew, by word of knowledge, the battle plans of the king of Syria (2Ki 6:12). This is just a sampling of miracles Elohim did through his human messengers before Yahushua came.

The point is, miracles do not prove deity. What they prove is the person has authority from above. The evidence is so clear that those saying miracles prove Yahushua is deity show how deceived they are. The Adversary has blinded their eyes. The doctrine of the deity of Christ is an idol in their hearts and they are worshiping (bowing down and giving homage to) it. It is a demonic stronghold within them. Brothers, you who are in this deception, wake up! Don't listen to the lie. Use the reason your Father created you with. That's why he gave it. Reject the "it's a mystery beyond reason" lie. Come out of Babylon.

Note what Yahushua said to the Jews who wanted to stone him.

> "Do not believe me unless I do what my Father does. But if I do it, even though you do not believe me, believe the miracles, that you may know and understand that the Father is in me, and I in the Father." (Jn 10:37-38, NIV)

Why were they wanting to stone him? He had said to them, *"I and the Father are one,"* (Jn 10:30). Then they accused him that he, a man (Gk *anthropos*), was making himself to be god/a god (Gk *theos*, Hb *elohim*). Then he reminded them that in their law it says, *"You are elohim,"* (Ps 82:6). Note: They were not accusing him of claiming to be the Almighty Elohim, but that he was making himself to be a *representative* of him, specifically the Messiah. That is the blasphemy for which they sentenced him to death at his trial.

When Yahushua said, *"I and the Father are one,"* (Jn 17:21-23), he was not claiming he was deity. He also prayed that believers in him be one in the same way that he and the Father are one (Jn 17:21-23). One what? One in being, that we all together be God? Of course not!

To be one with the Father means to be living in his will. This is what he prayed for us to be (Jn 17:21-23). In fact, this is the reason that was in the beginning; this is why we were created. This is what Paradise is. This is what Adam and Eve were before they sinned. And this is why Yahushua came, that he be the means whereby we can regain that Paradise. Only those who strive to be one with the Father and Yahushua as the Father and Yahushua are one can be in that Paradise (Php. 3:12-14).

I have read many Trinitarian writings, and a common statement is that Jesus was always claiming to be God. That is not true! Not once did Yahushua ever claim to be Elohim, never. It is nowhere in Scripture. He is always the son, a man, subordinated to Elohim. It is only in the minds of dual-naturists that everything he did and said proved he is deity. No! John declares what the miracles prove.

> But these are written that you may believe that Yahushua is **the** Messiah, **the** son of **the** Elohim, and that by believing you may have life in his name. (Jn 20:31, emphasis added to show the definite article in the Greek)

When Trinitarians see the phrase (the son of God), their mind changes it to "God the Son." Their minds are blinded to simple grammar and the rule of interpretation that says words must mean what they mean. In every other situation, for example, they can see that "the son of Bill" does not mean "Bill the son." But when it comes to the son of God, their brain sees or hears "God the Son." To them, that is the meaning of "the son of God."

I had a long discussion with a Trinitarian named Bill (a true story). He could see that "the son of Bill" is different from "Bill the son," but he couldn't see that the same grammar applied to "the son of God." Finally, after three hours of going over and over and over the same thing the deception left, he saw the difference, and he became a true monotheist.

The miracles of this man Yahushua included healing (the blind could see, the deaf could hear, the lame could walk, the dead came back to life, etc.) and casting out demons. This shows the authority he had over the curse of illness and death on man that resulted when Adam and Eve sinned.

But he had authority over nature as well. He changed water to wine (Jn 2:9). He walked on water, and so did Peter (Mt 14:25-29). He calmed the storm and raging sea (Mk 4:35-41). He cursed a fig tree so that it withered (Mk 11:12-14). He multiplied food (Mk 6:30-44; 8:1-13). He knew people's thoughts (Mt 9:4; Lk 9:47). He walked through crowds unseen (Lk 4:29-30). This is the authority Elohim gave to man. Yahushua said that if you have faith the size of a mustard seed you can tell a mountain to move from one place to another, and it will move; in fact, nothing will be impossible for you (Mt 17:20). He emphasized, "Truly, truly," meaning, take it literally.

Yahushua operated in seven of the gift manifestations[1] listed in 1 Corinthians 12:8-11. They are:

- Word of knowledge (Yahushua knowing their thoughts),
- Word of wisdom (knowing how to answer),
- Discernment of spirits (knowing what the demons were that he cast out),
- Miracles,
- Healings,
- Faith and
- Prophecy.

All these gift manifestations are given to humans, not to deities. They come from the Father to believers in Messiah for him to show himself to the world to draw people to him.

People used several titles regarding Yahushua. One is "son of God (Gk *theos*, Hb *elohim*). It is used 23 times in the Gospels, showing he has the character of the creator and is the Messiah. "Son of..." means character of.

In Luke 3:23-38 the genealogy of Yahushua starts with Joseph and ends with Adam who is "of God." Adam was created as an adult without any human father or mother. Yahushua began when a sperm created by Elohim fertilized an egg in Miryam. But Yahushua is more than a son by physical creation. He is **the** son of Yahuah because he bears his character.

"Son of David" is used 17 times in the Gospels for him, showing that he is a human descendent of king David and is the promised Messiah. "Son of Man" is used 82 times in the Gospels, showing that he represents mankind.

Here is a comparison of the authority of the last *adam*[2] with the first one before he sinned. The creation account in Genesis 1 mentions only authority over the animals. However, because he was living in total faith he could walk on water, play hide-and-seek with his wife (the only other human), multiply food, make a fruit drink out of water, and arrange the

---

1 Gk *charismata* = manifestations of favor (of Elohim).

2 Hb *adam* = man or mankind.

location of trees and plants with just a word. Although he had that ability, it likely never entered his mind to do so, for he was in unhindered fellowship with his Father and there was no need to do any of that. But we will never know. Yahushua did his miracles because of his ministry to confirm that he is the Messiah. What will it be like for us on the new earth with new bodies? Something to think about, and one day find out.

CHAPTER NINE

The Man Transfigured and Last Meal

———⊶∞⊷———

After six days Jesus took with him Peter, James and John the brother of James, and led them up a high mountain by themselves. There he was transfigured before them. His face shone like the sun, and his clothes became as white as the light. (Mt 17:1-3, NIV)

Transfiguration

WHAT HAPPENED in the transfiguration of Yahushua? Was he revealing his eternality, as those who believe in his eternality claim? We know this cannot be, for he is a man. And the infinite Yahuah cannot be a finite man, and a finite man cannot be the infinite Yahuah.

Rather, Yahuah was confirming to these three men that Yahushua is his chosen Messiah, and he was revealing the future esteem of his son after he would raise him from the dead, take him to heaven, and give him all authority in heaven and on earth. Yahuah was showing the importance of this man: *"This is my Son, whom I love; with him I am well pleased. Listen to him!"* (Mt 17:5, NIV).

Yahuah was emphasizing their relationship, his love for him, his pleasure in him, and the necessity to listen to him, with the desire to obey. To listen means joining your heart to what he says and listening with your heart and spirit so as to obey, for the words of this man Yahushua are the very words of Yahuah.

The two who were with Yahushua in the vision were Moses and Elijah. Moses represents the Law, and Elijah represents the Prophets. Together they represent the Old Covenant Scriptures. Both of them prophesied of Messiah. In this vision, the disciples saw the fulfillment of those prophecies, which would take place in the future after his resurrection and ascension. Yahushua is the greater Moses and the greater Elijah. They were men; so is Yahushua. Of note is what Moses told the children of Yisra'el about the Messiah to come: *"Yahuah your Elohim will raise up for you **a prophet like me from among your own brothers**. You must listen to him"* (Dt 18:15).

In this vision, Yahuah was saying to the disciples, "This is that man. He is your brother. He is my human son. He is the Messiah I promised. Listen to him."

Last meal

> For I received from the Lord what I also passed on to you: The Lord Jesus, on the night he was betrayed, took bread, and when he had given thanks, he broke it and said, "This is my body, which is for you; do this in remembrance of me." In the same way, after supper he took the cup, saying, "This cup is the new covenant in my blood; do this, whenever you drink it, in remembrance of me." For whenever you eat this bread and drink this cup, you proclaim the Lord's death until he comes. (1Cor 11:23-26, NIV)

This event must be looked at from the point of view that Yahushua was a man. He was a man, not a god-man but a human as we all are, who was about to become the slaughter offering for our sins, *"the lamb of Elohim that takes away the sin of the world"* (Jn 1:29). He qualified to be this offering because he never sinned and always pleased his Father.

It was the pagan reasoning of Athanasius at the Council of Nicea in C.E. 325, a council called by Emperor Constantine to bring unity in the church and thus in the empire, that won the vote among the select bishops that Constantine called to the meeting. The bishops were divided as to the nature of Christ.

By this time, 225 years after the New Testament was completed, the church had become gentile with many pagan practices and beliefs. All the bishops had come to believe that Messiah was a *theos* of some sort. The problem was, since Scripture says *theos* is one and the Father is *theos*, how can Messiah also be *theos*. That would make two *theoi*.[1]

The bishops of the West (Italy and North Africa) campaigned for Messiah to be *theos* equal with the Father. The bishops of the East (Greece, Palestine and eastward) campaigned for Messiah to be *a theos* created by the Father, so not equal with the Father.[2]

The champion debater of the West was Athanasius, a man educated in pagan Greek philosophy. He argued that no human blood could pay for man's sin. Even if that man were sinless, all he could do was pay for himself. Only the blood of *theos*, a *theos* equal with the Father, could pay for man's sin.

The East had no debater to match the skill of Athanasius, and the West won the vote. The West also won that the resurrection of Messiah be celebrated on the pagan day Easter Sunday, that the birth of Messiah be celebrated on the birthday of the sun-god Mithras, December 25, and that the weekly worship day be only on the sun-god day and not on the Sabbath 7th day.[3]

On the basis of that vote the emperor decreed that all churches must believe and practice the same, all dissenters be persecuted, and all contrary writings be burned. This was the beginning of orthodoxy and the Roman Catholic Church. This is why today's Christianity is in Babylon and why the doctrine of the Trinity defines Christianity instead of Scripture.

Trinitarian scholars today use that same reasoning of Athanasius: "Only divine blood can pay for man's sin, not human blood." That's why God had to become a man in order to have blood. If Jesus were only a

---

1 *Theos* and *theoi* are translated as "god" and "gods." At the meeting they spoke Greek, not Latin or English.

2 This belief is held by the Jehovah's Witnesses today.

3 At that time the churches in the west were meeting on the sun-god day and the churches in the east were meeting on Saturday. For believers in Messiah every day is a sabbath. Although we are commanded to meet together, the day to meet together is according to convenience. Christmas and Easter celebrations, however, are clearly pagan with no basis in Scripture.

man and not also God then his blood would be no different from any other human martyr who died for his belief. Lie, LIE, **LIE!!!** Horrible, wicked, evil, monstrous!

Trinitarians sincerely believe this while loving Jesus and God. I weep for them in their deception. I pray that their eyes be opened to see how horrible and wicked a lie it is. They are in the grip of Satan, at least in this belief and in its effect regarding salvation. Although it is not a salvation issue at this time, the day will come when it will be a salvation issue. For Yahushua is coming for a bride without spot or wrinkle, and this doctrine is a very large spot and wrinkle. Those who do not come out will miss the rapture and go through the great tribulation in which they must either die for their faith or lose their salvation. How soon that day will come no one knows but, as both John and Yahushua proclaimed: *"Repent, for the kingdom of heaven is near."* Repent means to change.

Now back to that last meal.

> "I tell you the truth, unless you eat the flesh of the Son of Man and drink his blood, you have no life in you. Whoever eats my flesh and drinks my blood has eternal life, and I will raise him up at the last day. For my flesh is real food and my blood is real drink. Whoever eats my flesh and drinks my blood remains in me, and I in him." (Jn 6:53-56, NIV)

The bread symbolizes that our daily food is serving Yahushua and living for him in all we do. This is how we "eat his flesh." And the cup symbolizes his blood that was shed for our sin. *"Without the shedding of blood there is no forgiveness"* (Heb 9:22).

> For God is one; and there is but one Mediator between God and humanity, Yeshua the Messiah, himself human, who gave himself as a ransom on behalf of all. (1Ti 2:5-6, CJB)

Man sinned, man must die (Eze 18:20). God did not and cannot sin and he has no blood, nor can he become a finite man to have blood. Yahushua, the last *adam,* represents mankind. Because this man died for us he is the mediator between Elohim and us. We can never, throughout all eternity, come into the presence of Yahuah directly. Forever Yahushua is our mediator and the means whereby we have fellowship with the Father (Jn 14:6,9; Ac 4:12. Rev 21:23). Because Elohim said that this man's blood covers our sin, then that decides it. No reasoning of Athanasius and Trinitarians has the power to change Scripture.

Conclusion

It was a man, a man only, who was transfigured. And it was the blood of a man, a man only, that covers our sin. However, keep in mind that that covering only works as long as we repent of sin and take up our cross to overcome sin daily (Lk 9:23). Security in salvation is eternal when we have endured to the end (Mt 24:13). We can lose it any time we turn away.

I [Paul] discipline my body and bring *it* into subjection, lest ... I myself should become disqualified. (1Cor 9:27, NKJ)

CHAPTER TEN

The Coming Spirit of Set-apartness[1]

———⧟———

"I will ask the Father, and he will give you another *parakletos* (Greek)/ Counselor (NIV)/ Helper (NAS)/ Advocate (NRS) to be with you forever." (Jn 14:16)

JOHN CHAPTERS 14-17 RECORD THE LAST TEACHINGS of Yahushua during his last meal before his arrest. In these teachings he is preparing the disciples for the coming spirit of set-apartness. After his resurrection and just before his ascension to heaven, he said, *"You shall receive power when the spirit of set-apartness comes on you, and you shall be my witnesses."*[2] Soon after, on the Day of Pentecost, the spirit came and the assembly was born. It began with power, signs, wonders and anointed teaching that convicted people of their sins so they would repent, believe that Yahushua is the Messiah, the son of Elohim, and enter his kingdom.

The disciples didn't want Yahushua to die; they wanted him to stay with them and establish the kingdom on earth. They were looking for an earthly kingdom. They, along with all the other Jews, did not understand that the Messiah needed to die for their sins, that he was the fulfillment of all the Old Testament sacrifices.

---

1 The spirit of set-apartness includes all the moral attributes of Yahuah: love, goodness, righteousness, impartial justice, compassion, mercy, favor, wisdom, counsel, strength, faithfulness, fear of Yahuah, hatred of evil, jealousy to protect his own, etc.
2 Ac 1:8.

Because Yahushua was sinless he was in complete union with the Father. They were one in the sense that Yahushua lived completely in the will of Yahuah. They moved in perfect harmony—the Father in him and he in the Father. The Father is spirit and he created us for us to be his dwelling place, he living in us and we living in him. Yahushua had this relationship, and his death for our sins made it possible for us to have this relationship also—we in the Father and son and they in us (Jn 17:21-23). Until his death for our sins it was impossible for us to be reconciled with the Father and for him to dwell in us. It is only because of Messiah's death for our sins that we can have the kind of fellowship with the Father that Yahushua had.

When Yahushua left the Jordan after his immersion by John and was led into the desert to be tempted he had the spirit of Yahuah fully, or, to put it in another way, the Father dwelt in him fully, as fully as it is possible for the infinite Elohim to dwell in a human. During his three-and-a-half years' ministry he operated in the fullness of the Father's spirit. Therefore, while he was with the disciples physically, the spirit of set-apartness in him was *with* them, but could not be *in* them until the offering of his life was complete. When that happened, then he could send the spirit to them, which would begin the assembly. That's what happened at Pentecost. That's why he said to them, *"I will ask the Father, and he will give you **another** helper to be with you forever"* (Jn 14:16, NAS). The Father was *with* them in Yahushua, but after Pentecost he would be *in* them directly.

Many dwelling places

> "In My Father's house are many dwelling places; ... If I go and prepare a place for you, I will come again and receive you to Myself, that where I am, *there* you may be also. (Jn 14:2-3, NASU)

These words introduce the subject of the spirit of set-apartness that would dwell in them. The traditional understanding of this passage is that Yahushua was talking about life in heaven after death. But that is totally out of context. The context is the coming spirit of set-apartness. What is the Father's house? It is people who love and obey him.

Thus says Yahuah, "The heavens are my throne and the earth is my footstool. Where is a **dwelling place** that you could build for me? And where is a place that I may rest? For my hand made all these things. ... But to this one I will look, to him who is humble and contrite of spirit, and who trembles at my word." (Is 66:1-2)

You also, like living stones, are being built into **a spiritual house** to be a set-apart priesthood, offering spiritual sacrifices acceptable to Elohim through Yahushua Messiah. (1Per 2:5)

The many dwelling places are believers in whom the Father dwells. He is the spirit of set-apartness.

Parakletos.[2] *"I will ask the Father, and he will give you another parakletos"* (Jn 14:16). One of the most misunderstood teachings of Yahushua is what he said about the *parakletos*. The word means: "legal adviser, advocate, counselor, helper."[3] It is a legal term, like a lawyer in a court case. It is made up of two Greek words: *para* (alongside) and *kaléo* (to call). Put together as a participle in one word it means "one called alongside," namely, to help in any of those four capacities listed above in the definition.

In 1 John 2:1 it is used for our exalted righteous Yahushua as a *parakletos* (advocate) before the Father in the event we sin. Without his advocacy our periodic sin cannot be forgiven. Forever he is our mediator before the Father, and because of that the Father can look through him to us. Our Father's plan for this man for our salvation is too wonderful for words.

The four other times *parakletos* is used is in these last teachings of Yahushua to refer to the spirit of set-apartness as the helper. They are John 14:15-20; 14:26; 15:26 and 16:5-14. Although *parakletos* (helper) is a masculine noun in Greek, because in these passages it refers to *pneuma* (spirit) which is neuter, and because the spirit of set-apartness of Yahuah is not a person but an "it" just as your spirit is an "it" and not a person, the neuter pronoun "it" is used. This is the same principle as when we

---

2 Trinitarians call the Third Person of the Trinity "The Paraklete."

3 Strong's # 3875, Exegetical Dictionary of the New Testament

discussed *logos* (word). Although it is a masculine noun, it is not a person, so in English it is neuter and takes the neuter pronoun "it."

In these verses Yahushua says these things about the helper.

1) Receiving it depends on obedience. (Jn 14:15)
2) Yahushua asks the Father to give it to us and
3) the Father gives it. (Jn 14:16)
4) It is another helper different from himself. (Jn 14:16)
5) The helper is to be with us forever. (Jn 14:16)
6) The helper is the spirit of the truth.[4] (Jn 14:17)
7) The world cannot accept the helper because it neither sees it nor knows it. (Jn 14:17)
8) The disciples know the helper because it lives with them and will be in them. (Jn 14:17)
9) Yahushua will not leave them as orphans but will come to them. (Jn 14:18)
10) The world won't see Yahushua anymore, but the disciples will. (Jn 14:19)
11) Because Yahushua lives, they will live. (Jn 14:19)
12) On that day they will realize that Yahushua is in his Father, and they are in him, and he is in them. (Jn 14:20)
13) The helper is the spirit of set-apartness. (Jn 14:26)
14) The Father will send the helper in the name of Yahushua. (Jn 14:26)
15) The helper will teach them all things and will remind them of everything Yahushua said to them. (Jn 14:26)
16) Yahushua will send the helper to them from the Father. (Jn 15:26)
17) The helper is the spirit of the truth. (Jn 15:26)
18) The helper goes out from the Father. (Jn 15:26)
19) The helper will testify about Yahushua. (Jn 15:26)
20) Yahushua is going to the Father who sent him. (Jn 16:5)
21) It is for their good that Yahushua is going away because the helper can't come unless he does. (Jn 16:7)
22) When Yahushua goes he will send the helper to them. (Jn 16:7)

---

4 Both "spirit" and "truth" have the definite article.

23) When the helper comes it will convict the world of guilt for sin, righteousness and judgment. (Jn 16:8)
24) When the spirit of the truth comes it will guide them into all truth. (Jn 16:13)
25) The spirit of the truth will not speak on its own but only what it hears. (Jn 16:13)
26) The spirit of the truth will tell them what is yet to come. (Jn 16:13)
27) The spirit of the truth will bring esteem to Yahushua by taking from what is his and making it known to them. (Jn 16:14)

That's quite a list and it has some very interesting things in it. All of this happens because of the Father in Messiah dwelling in believers who are obedient to him. It is by *Elohim's* spirit that the finite son of *Elohim*, a man now having all authority in heaven and on earth, is able to have fellowship with the whole assembly world-wide at the same time (Jn 14:18,26; 15:26).

Other verses in John

John 14:28

"The Father is greater than I."

The Father is greater than the son because the Father is *Elohim* and his son is a man. All that Yahushua did was because of the Father in him. The oneness of man with *Elohim* doesn't make man **Elohim**. Man is the manifestation of *Elohim*; *Elohim* is the one doing the manifestation in cooperation with the man yielding himself to *Elohim*.

John 14:30

"The prince of this world ... has no hold on me."

Throughout Yahushua's ministry the devil could find nothing in this man that he could use to draw him into sin. Nothing. What a testimony! The more we become like Yahushua, the less we become like the devil.

John 17:3

"Now this is eternal life: that they may know you, the only true Elohim, and Yahushua Messiah, whom you have sent."

Yahushua said the Father is the only true Elohim. And he identified himself as a separate being from this only true Elohim. All the Scriptures must be interpreted according to this revelation, including the Gospel of John that contains these words of Yahushua.

What about 1 John 5:20 which says the *son* of Elohim is "the true God and eternal life" (NIV)? The son can be called *elohim* because he represents Elohim. However, when we look at it in a more literal translation we get a better explanation.

"But we know that the son of Elohim has come, and he has given us understanding, so **that we may know the true one**. And we are **in** the true one in/by means of his son Yahushua Messiah. **This** is the true Elohim and eternal life." (1Jn 5:20)

Who is "the true one" that the son of Elohim is giving us understanding about? Is it not Elohim the Father? We are in *"the true one"* by being in his son Yahushua Messiah. The word "This" is a demonstrative pronoun. Is the word "This" referring to Elohim, or to his son, or to Elohim in his son?

The whole context of John's writings is *Elohim* in his son. John is emphasizing that the only true Elohim is the one in his son, Yahushua Messiah; he will not be found anywhere else. And therefore the only eternal life is by being in his son. Elohim is in his son, and we are in Elohim by means of being in his son. In another sense, however, we can say the son is the true Elohim, for the Father and son are one. But this does not make him more than a human only.

John 17:5

"And now esteem me, Father, alongside yourself with the esteem (glory) which I was having alongside you before the world came to be."

The Greek word for "world" in this verse is *kosmos*. *Kosmos* in the New Testament is used in two basic ways: a few times referring to the physical universe, and the great majority of times to fallen mankind and the resultant system of which Satan is the ruler (Jn 16:11). Commentaries written by Trinitarians take the word *kosmos* in the first basic sense, so they interpret this verse to mean Messiah existed before the creation of the physical universe, and he gave up the esteem he had in that position when he became a man. And so, these commentators say, Yahushua is praying to get that esteem back after his death and resurrection.

This cannot be the meaning, because Yahushua never existed before he was born, so he never had that esteem. Further, according to Trinitarian theology, the Second Person of the god-essence never lost his esteem.

So we must go by the second and majority meaning: the world system of fallen man. In this prayer Yahushua is praying on behalf of mankind. He is the last Adam. The first Adam had esteem with the Father before he sinned, an esteem in which he operated fully in the Father's will, and an esteem in which Yahushua operated. But when the first Adam fell, that esteem was lost and the world system of fallen man began (Ro 3:23). Elohim gave his son to save fallen man (Jn 3:16). Yahushua is praying that that esteem which man had in the Garden before the fall be regained. The whole context of this prayer is about this.

John 17:11

"And I am no more in the world, but these are in the world, and I come to you, set-apart Father, **guard them in your Name which you have given me**, so that they might be one, as we are."

The Father's name has power. In the OT it is Yahuah. He gave his name to his son. It is Yahushua, which means "Yahuah is salvation." This is the New Covenant name of Yahuah. The assembly has yet to receive the full revelation of the name of Yahushua. It has power to protect us, and power to make us one as a body in the same way that the Father and son are one. When we say the name Yahushua, we are saying the name of the Father and the son. Yahuah wants us to be immersed in that name. He wants that name to be our life. The Father is in the son, and the son is in the Father. They are one, and the name Yahushua can apply to them both as one.

John 17:21-23

"...that all of them may be one, Father, just as you are in me and I am in you. May they also be in us so that the world may believe that you have sent me. I have given them the esteem that you gave me, that they may be one as we are one: I in them and you in me. May they be perfected into one to let the world know that you sent me and have loved them even as you have loved me."

The oneness that Yahushua had with the Father was not oneness of being, but oneness of heart, soul, and mind, and by the means of this oneness the life of the Father could operate in him fully. This passage shows Yahuah in Messiah and how he wants Messiah to be in us. This is the prayer of Yahushua for the bride. Only the bride will fulfill this. Those who desire to be a part of the bride should also have this as their constant prayer.

Note: Yahushua prayed that believers in him be one *in the same way that he and the Father are one.* Because no one of us is one in three, neither is he. Believers in the "deity" of Messiah totally miss what Yahushua is praying about. When we understand that Yahushua is a man in whom the one Elohim (the Father) dwelt fully, as Yahushua taught, then we are in position to get the revelation of this prayer.

This is a powerful prayer. Words are not capable of describing its full impact. It birthed the assembly through immersion in the spirit of set-apartness and set in motion the perfection of the called-out-ones to produce a remnant bride to have the same relationship with one another and with the Father and son that the Father and son have. It is a union of soul and spirit so complete that all become one operational body, moving in the spirit without any hindrance. It is a union that enables the Father to manifest himself fully any way he wants. It is a union with power and effectiveness never before seen on earth. It is a union that will destroy the antichrist world government (although the antichrist world government will revive after the bride is raptured). One cannot enter into this relationship and this union unless he also understands the relationship of the Father and son—for we are to have that same relationship. It is a relationship of Yahuah—Elohim the Father— fully in a man.

Conclusion

Yahuah, who is the set-apart spirit, created us humans to be in his image and likeness so that he could live in us forever. Because we sinned we could not have that relationship but deserve eternal separation from him, called hell. But he knew there would be a man, conceived miraculously without a human father, who would be like the first man before he sinned and who would not sin. This man would be his special son in a special relationship. His plan was to offer this darling of his heart to die in our place so our sin could be forgiven and we be restored to the position of fellowship that the first man had. When the payment for our sin was completed, then the Father could dwell in us. This is the spirit of set-apartness. This is what Yahushua was teaching about during his last meal before his execution for our sins. This is why he said it was good for them that he go away.

CHAPTER ELEVEN

The Man from Garden to Resurrection

———∽∾∝∾———

"Father, if you are willing, take this cup from me; yet not my will, but yours be done." (Lk 22:42, NIV)

Gethsemane

T HIS WAS YAHUSHUA'S FINAL TEST BEFORE BEING impaled.

During the days of his flesh he offered up prayers and petitions with loud cries and tears to the one who could save him from death, and he was heard because of his reverent fear. Although he was a son, he learned obedience from what he suffered and, once made complete, he became the source of eternal salvation for all who obey him and was designated by Elohim to be high priest in the order of Melchizedek. (Heb 5:7-10.)

As it is with all humans, throughout Yahushua's life he was being tested. This was the final and hardest test of this man. Every test we pass prepares the way for the next test a bit harder. In this test we see a man being asked to do something that he didn't want to do. His whole being cringed at the thought. His was a human will having to decide whether to accept the test or reject it. The accounts don't say what he was being asked to do.

73

If he were the Second Person of a god-essence trinity, his will would be the same as the First Person. Trinitarians get around this by saying his 100% humanity had a human will that was separate from his 100% deity will. So his humanity side didn't want to do what his divinity side wanted to do.

> Schizophrenia. n. Behavior that appears to be motivated by contradictory or conflicting principles. (Collins English Dictionary)

"I am" and they fell to the ground.

When the temple guards led by Judas came to the garden looking for Yahushua, and he told them *"I, I am,"* they went backward and fell to the ground (Jn 18:4-6).

Trinitarians believe this incident shows the deity of Yahushua. Wrong. Again, they are reading their theology into the happening. The Greek for "I, I am" is *ego* (I) *eimi* (I am). (Adding the pronoun "I" gives emphasis.) They say that by this statement he was saying that he is the "I AM" that Yahuah spoke to Moses (Ex 3:14). Wrong again. In English if someone asks you if you are so-and-so and you respond by saying "I am," everyone knows you are not claiming to be the "I AM" creator of the universe. They know you mean "I am that person." The same is true in the Greek of the New Testament for others as well as Yahushua.

"But," Trinitarians reply, "they fell down. That shows he is deity." Wrong still again. This shows that the power of his Father was present when Yahushua identified himself as the one they were looking for. It was also an opportunity for the priests to repent of their hard-heartedness. This is the kind of power Yahuah wants believers in Yahushua to have. I personally have seen hundreds of people fall under the power of the spirit of set-apartness during evangelistic healing meetings. Does that mean the speaker is deity?

Tried and sentenced

> The high priest said to him, "I put you to oath, by the living Elohim that you **say to us if you are the Messiah, the son of Elohim**."

Yahushua said to him, "You have said it. Besides I say to you, from now you shall see the son of Adam sitting at **the right hand of the Power**,[1] and coming on the clouds of the heaven." Then the high priest tore his garments, saying, "He has blasphemed! Why do we need any more witnesses? See, now you have heard his blasphemy! "What do you think?" And they answering, said, "He is liable to death." (Mt 26:63-66)

What blasphemy was Yahushua accused of at his trial before the high priest? And what did Yahushua say about himself that so angered them that they took him to Pilate to be executed? Did he claim to be Elohim? Or did he claim to be a man who was the son of Elohim (a title for the Messiah)? The charge against Yahushua in the Matthew account is that he claimed to be the son of *Elohim* and the Sovereign of Yisra'el. Note: he did not claim, nor did he ever claim, to *be Elohim*.[2]

Nowhere in the trial was he ever accused of claiming to *be* Elohim, only of claiming to be the **son of** *Elohim*. They were true monotheists (believers in one Elohim who is one), who believed the Father is the only true Elohim. If they thought Yahushua were claiming to be the *Elohim*, you can be sure they would have brought it up at the trial. But they never did! It is only those who believe Messiah is the *Elohim* (along with two other Persons) who believe he claimed to be *Elohim*, for they don't believe in his true humanity. They call it "humanity," but it is not, for it is different from all other humans.

Forsaken, Matthew 27:46

"Eli, eli, lama sabachthani?" that is, "My El, my El, why have you forsaken me?"

What died on the stake? Was it a man, a God-man, or God? Trinitarians say God had to die for us, that only the death of God could atone for our

1 "The Power" was a substitute word for Yahuah, the ineffable Name not to be spoken.

2 See Mt 27:42-43 for the accusations against him while he was on the stake. (We don't know if the post had a crosspiece.)

sins. As noted before, that's not what Yahuah says. Yahuah is immortal, and immortal means cannot die. Trinitarians get around this problem by saying, "Yahuah took on mortality so he *could* die for us. After all, Yahuah is omnipotent. He can do anything." Wrong! There are some things Yahuah cannot do. Here are four.

- He cannot stop being Elohim.
- He cannot change into something he is not.
- He cannot change his nature.
- He cannot become finite to be part of his creation.

On the stake Yahushua prayed, *"My El, my El, why have you forsaken me?"* Can one Elohim have another Elohim as his Elohim? Where is the equality here? And can Elohim be forsaken? It was the son of Elohim, a man, who died. He lived a totally sinless life, pleasing his Father always. Yahuah took this man, his darling beloved son, and offered him to be killed as a lamb slaughter for our sins. Yahuah put the guilt of our sins upon him, and then withdrew his presence. Then Yahushua surrendered his spirit to his Father and died.

Finished

On the stake Yahushua said, *"It is finished,"* then gave up his spirit (Jn 19:30). What was finished? Did the eternal Elohim give up his spirit, as Trinitarians claim? *Elohim* is spirit; how can he give up his existence? It was a man, a creation of *Elohim*, the darling of Yahuah's heart, who gave up his spirit. This man finished paying the offering that we might have salvation through his blood, so he left his body and went to Paradise (Lk 23:43).

Resurrected

When Yahushua said to the Jews, *"Destroy this temple, and in three days I will raise it up"* (Jn 2:19), he was speaking of his death and resurrection. This brings up the question: Who raised him from the dead? Acts 2:24 and Galatians 1:1 say it was the Father. Romans 8:11 says it was the spirit of Elohim. And John 2:19 and 10:17-18 say he raised himself up. From

John 14:10 we learn that the only way Yahushua did (and does) anything supernatural was (and is) the Father in him doing it. Man cannot do miracles. But Yahuah in man can.

Is Yahuah confused in what he inspired to be written? How Trinitarians try to fit this into their theology is too mixed up to relate. When one uses words of Yahuah as the only source of truth, and not creeds from paganized church councils, the answer is simple. In Romans 8:9,11 it says *"the spirit of Elohim."*

The Father by the power of his spirit raised his son from the dead. The words of Yahushua in John 10:17-18 make it clear that it was by the authority of the Father that he raised his body from the dead, just as it was the Father's authority that enabled him to raise others from the dead. (And just as it was the Father's authority that enabled Peter and Paul to raise the dead.) Although the body of Yahushua was dead, he was alive in Paradise (Lk 23:43). Man cannot do miracles, but Elohim in man can. Yahuah wants to give us the same authority he gave his son.

"My Father and your Father"

After his resurrection Yahushua told Mary to tell his brothers, *"I am ascending to my Father and your Father, and to my Elohim and your Elohim"* (Jn 20:17). This says the Father is Elohim of Yahushua in the same way that he is our Elohim. Of course he says this, because he is a human the same as we are.

"My Master and my elohim"

Yahushua appeared to the disciples several times after his resurrection. During one of those times Thomas said to him, *"My Master and my elohim!"* (Jn 20:28). What did he mean by this? There are several possibilities, all of which could be true.

- He could be speaking to Yahushua as Master and to the Father in him as Elohim, the two as one.
- He could be calling Yahushua elohim in the sense that he fully represents Elohim and therefore is his elohim. (see Heb 1:8-9).

- Messiah is in such a high position that the only term that can adequately express this man is Elohim.
- When Thomas saw Yahushua, he saw past the man to Elohim in him and spoke directly to the Father. The Father and son are one. You cannot separate them.

Written that ...

These have been written so that you believe that Yahushua is the Messiah, the son of Elohim, and that, believing, you might possess life in his name. (Jn 20:31)

All that John included in his Gospel was for one purpose: to reveal Yahushua as the Messiah and the son of Yahuah Elohim, a man fully one with his Father, in order that by believing we may have life in his name. The union of Elohim and his son is so intimate and complete they cannot be separated. This is the way Yahuah Elohim wants it with us.

Conclusion

Everything we have seen about Messiah—from Old Testament prophecy, through his life on earth, death and resurrection—is about a man, not a god-man.

CHAPTER TWELVE

The Man As High Priest

—❦—

"All authority in heaven and on earth has been given to me." (Mt 28:18)

The Master Yahushua ... was taken up into heaven and he sat at the right hand of Elohim. Then the disciples went out and preached everywhere, and the Master worked with them and confirmed his word by the signs that accompanied it. (Mk 16:19-20)

Because Yahushua lives forever, he has a permanent priesthood. Therefore he is able to save completely those who come to Elohim through him, because he always lives to intercede for them. (Heb 7:24-25)

The right hand

AFTER YAHUSHUA ASCENDED TO HEAVEN HE SAT at the right hand of Elohim. The scripture verses that say this are too numerous to list here. They are in fulfillment of the prophecy of David about the Messiah in Psalm 110:1.[1]

Trinitarians are tritheists (believing there are three Gods) while saying they are monotheists (believing there is only one God). Their explanation of Yahushua at the right hand of God demonstrates this. When

---

1 See also 1 Peter 3:21-22.

they picture in their minds all of God, they have God the Father on a throne sitting in the middle, God the Son sitting on his right side, and God the Holy Spirit sitting on his left side or hovering over them as a cloud or ghost. Count them. That's three. Each is fully and equally all of God with all the attributes of God. The one on the right-hand side left his position on the throne in order to become a human, while still being God. By this act, God (i.e. God the Son and also the Trinity) changed, without changing (for God cannot change). After his death and resurrection, he again resumed his seat at the right-hand side of the Father. This time, though, he is a God-man.

How can this be? Elohim is infinite, omnipresent, invisible spirit filling heaven and earth. It is impossible for him to be on the right side of himself literally. The language is figurative, and visions of him are pictorial because of our finite understanding. Where in the Scriptures is the Holy Spirit said to be on the left side of Elohim or a cloud? This is all the result of false doctrine from paganism.

In all the verses of Yahushua at the right hand of Elohim, it is a man whom the Father exalted to a position of authority. The right hand of Elohim is the name of that position. "Right-hand" is a figure of speech for authority. Right-hand means "most helpful or reliable," such as "the president's right-hand man." We, the assembly of Messiah, are supposed to be in that position also.

Advocate

> My little children, I am writing these things to you so that you may not sin. And if anyone sins, we have an advocate *(parakletos)* with the Father, Yahushua Messiah the righteous; and he himself is the propitiation for our sins; and not for ours only, but also for the whole world. (1Jn 2:1-2)

It is a man who is our advocate, the one who intercedes for us.

> There is one Elohim and one mediator between Elohim and men, the **man** Yahushua Messiah, who gave himself as a ransom for all men. (1Ti 2:5-6)

Everywhere with us

"I, I am with you all the days, to the completion of the age." (Mt 28:20)

This is an amazing promise. How can a finite man be everywhere at the same time? Isn't that the prerogative of infinite deity? Isn't this statement evidence of his deity? What about the statement that finite man cannot become infinite?

Let us look at this "impossibility" in another way. What can we humans do here on earth without any help from inventions? Very little. But with inventions we can drive cars, fly around the earth and to the moon, communicate with the speed of light, etc.

Yahushua said, *"With Elohim all things are possible"* (Mt 19:26). Yahuah is present everywhere all the time, past, present and future. Yahushua (and all believers who have died) are no longer in their earthly physical bodies. They are in a condition we know nothing about. Is not Elohim who created this physical universe by speaking the word, who parted the Red Sea and made water gush forth from solid rock, who has raised the dead—is he not able to enable a finite man to be everywhere at once on this earth, and also to be everywhere in time, past, present and future?

Yahushua was given all authority in heaven and on earth. Note: It was *given* to him. He didn't have it until it was given to him. If he were deity, then he would have it by virtue of his nature and wouldn't need it to be given to him. But he is finite man, so it had to be given to him. And how could he have all authority unless he had the knowledge and ability to exercise that authority? It would have to be Yahuah giving him that knowledge and ability.

When we pray for others, interceding for them, we do so on the basis of our finite knowledge and any "word of knowledge" Messiah might give us. Consider all the billions of people on earth. Yahushua, a finite man, is interceding for them all, all the time. He can do that because his Father is in him giving him all the information he needs. That includes knowing everything about everyone all the time, past, present and future.

Ladies and gentlemen, readers of this book, we have no idea what the situation will be for believers in Messiah after we die. But it will be wonderful beyond our present comprehension. That is our retirement, not this earth. We say, "You can't take it with you." There is no physical thing here I want to take with me, only relationships.

Conclusion

I am so thankful that there is a man who never sinned, a man who gave up his life for us, and a man who therefore could be in the exalted authority he has. It is because of this man, what he did and was, that he is the reason for creation. Without him there would be no creation and no one of us would exist.

CHAPTER THIRTEEN

The Man Returns With His Bride

The man returns

"But in those days, after that tribulation, ... they will see the Son of Man coming in the clouds with great power and glory." (Mk 13:24, 26, NKJV)

THESE VERSES REFER TO THE SECOND COMING of Messiah to establish his 1000-year rule, called the Millennium. Our topic doesn't include a detailed examination of that rule, but a brief overview will set the stage.

Mark 13 is often called "the Little Apocalypse"[1] because in it Yahushua summarizes the end-time events. John's vision recorded in the Book of Revelation goes into more detail. After the rapture (Rev 12:5) believers who miss it will have the choice of being martyred to keep their salvation, or take the mark of the beast (666) and lose their salvation (Rev 13). This period is called the Great Tribulation and lasts 3½ years and ends the 2000-year Gentile Age of the Church. No believers remain on earth, for all have either been raptured or martyred.

Seven plagues come on mankind shortly after this, lasting another 3½ years.[2] These plagues are judgments on the people for killing all

---

1 Apocalypse = revelation. The Book of Revelation is often called the Apocalypse.

2 The 3½ years of tribulation on believers and the 3½ years of plagues on mankind make up the seven years of Great Tribulation.

the believers and for refusing to repent. The seventh plague is what is popularly called "the Battle of Armageddon" in which Satan's one-world government brings the armies of all nations against Jerusalem.

This battle against Jerusalem is the final event in which the Jews finally realize their only hope is in Yahuah their Elohim and they call out to him for help and repent of their hardheartedness (Joel 2:15-18).

In answer to their prayer and repentance, Yahushua returns and destroys the armies that have come against Jerusalem. He destroys almost all the people on earth and destroys all their cities and has Satan and his demons bound for 1000 years so they can do nothing to mankind. This is the end of the seventh and last plague. Only a handful in each nation remain alive to enter the Millennium. Israel becomes the head nation of the world with Jerusalem the capital. When Yahushua comes he is not alone, but all believers from Adam to the end of the Gentile age will come with him. These are the ones who will rule the earth with Messiah during the 1000 years.

After the 1000 years is up, according to the Book of Revelation, the following things happen:

1) Satan and his demons are released.
2) Most of mankind follow him.
3) They come against Jerusalem again in the final battle on earth.
4) Yahushua ends it killing all the wicked and taking the believers to heaven leaving no humans on earth.
5) Satan and his demons are thrown into hell.
6) The universe is dissolved with fire.
7) The final judgment begins in which each person is judged according to what he has done in his life.
8) The wicked are sent to hell with their varying degrees of judgment.
9) And the righteous, called the bride of Messiah, inherit the new heaven and new earth with their varying degrees of reward.

With that as the background we want to examine two verses about Messiah's coming and the reaction of the Jews in seeing him. Except for a very small remnant, the Jews have never accepted that Yahushua is their Messiah. Their whole history, beginning with the Hebrews leaving Egypt, is one of rebellion against Yahuah their Elohim by being involved in idolatry. But now, after seeing the powerful miracles done in the name of Yahushua Messiah by the last-day perfected assembly (Jn 14:12-14) and rejecting that, and then realizing that they are losing against the huge army coming against them, a remnant of them cry out to Yahuah for help. And then they see Yahuah/Yahushua coming down in a cloud.

"They will look on me [Yahuah], the one they have pierced, and they will mourn for him as one mourns for an only child, and grieve bitterly for him as one grieves for a firstborn son." (Zec 12:10, NIV)

BEHOLD, HE IS COMING WITH THE CLOUDS, and every eye will see Him, even those who pierced Him; and all the tribes of the earth will mourn over Him. (Rev 1:7, NASU)

In Zechariah's prophesy Yahuah says he is the one whom they see, whom they pierced and who is coming. In Revelation it is Messiah. Is this a contradiction? No. It is a revelation. Yahuah is spirit and cannot be pierced physically. Yahuah who created emotions has emotions. He can be angry and sad as well as be pleased and happy. Even as we can wound one another with words and actions, so we can wound our creator. When Yahushua was pierced physically for our sin, Yahuah was pierced emotionally. Every sin we do hurts our Father.

Seldom do we wound others physically, but all too often we wound them with words and actions. Those of tender hearts, when they realize they have hurt someone, repent and feel remorse. When Messiah returns, the demon bondage of hardness of heart will be gone and the people will repent with deep sob-wrenching sorrow for all their wickedness. These are the ones who are left alive when the Millennium begins.

One other observation: When Yahushua comes his Father will be in him. No one can see the Father; the only way we can see him is in his human son. *"He who has seen me as seen the Father"* (Jn 14:9).

The bride of Yahuah/Yahushua

We have talked much in this book about the bride of Messiah. Who is the husband of the bride? In Isaiah 54:5-6 Yahuah says he is the husband of Yisra'el and Yisra'el is his wife. Yet in Revelation 21:9 we see the bride is the wife of the Lamb, the Lamb referring to Yahushua Messiah (Rev 19-22).

The nation of Yisra'el is a type of (symbolic of) the assembly of Messiah. The bride is a group of people including both male and female, not an individual person. The terms bride, wife, bridegroom, and husband are symbolic of the relationship that our Father wants with us. And that relationship is through his human son, Yahushua.

CHAPTER FOURTEEN

All For The Father

—◦◦◦—

Then the end, when he delivers up the kingdom to Elohim and Father, when he has abolished all rule and all authority and power. For he must reign until he has put all his enemies under his feet. The last enemy that will be abolished is death. For he has put all things in subjection under his feet. But when he says, "All things are put in subjection," it is evident that he is excepted who put all things in subjection to him. When all things are subjected to him, then the son himself also will be subjected to the one who subjected all things to him, **so that Elohim may be all in all.** (1Cor 15:24-28)

THESE VERSES SHOW THE SUBORDINATION OF THE son to the Father. There is no equality here, nor has there ever been, because the son is a created human being as we all are. The *"all authority in heaven and on earth"* (Mt 28:18) that the Father gave him is temporary. When his job is finished he gives all that authority back to the Father.

The letters of Paul to the assemblies all show that everything is done for the Father *through* the son. The son is forever our mediator. We will look at Romans as an example. This letter—the so-called "theology book" of Paul—is like an introduction to all his other letters. The other letters have the same message regarding the relationship of Elohim and the human Messiah. The following passage is an example of the others.

The righteousness of Elohim is through belief in Yahushua Messiah to all and on all who believe. For there is no difference, for all have sinned and fall short of the esteem of Elohim, being declared right, without paying, by his favor through the redemption which is in [his human Son] Messiah Yahushua. (Ro 3:22-24, brackets added)

What follows is a summary of Romans. Elohim is the source of the good news regarding the Messiah. It is Elohim's good news. His son by birth is descended from David. Although the miracles he did showed Elohim was in him and that he is the promised Messiah, the final and greatest proof that he is *the* son of Elohim as no other man is or ever will be, is his resurrection from the dead with great power by the spirit of set-apartness. It is through this man—and this man alone—that Elohim brings salvation to mankind. Favor and peace come to us from the two—Elohim our Father and the human Master Yahushua Messiah. Consistently, Paul gives thanks *to* the Father *through* the human mediator, Yahushua Messiah. Paul serves Elohim by preaching the good news of his son. For that preaching is the power of Elohim to save everyone who believes. It saves because it reveals a righteousness from Elohim. (Ro 1:1-4, 7-9; 1:16-17; 3:22-24; 15:5-7)

Throughout Scripture the message is the same: The Father is the only true Elohim, his spirit is himself, and his son is a man in whom Elohim lived fully so that the two are one (Jn 17:21-23). Because of this union he is called the word of Elohim. To see the son is to see Elohim, for the son is the soul, heart, purpose and plan (word) of Elohim made flesh, and thus he can be called Elohim (the strong one). This is the meaning of indwelling in the Scriptures, namely, Elohim *in* flesh.

This finishes "Part One: The Man" in which we have looked at the life of the man Yahushua Messiah and have seen that according to Scripture he is a man only. We now go to "Part Two: Other Verses."

In Part Two we look at Rules of Interpretation and then, by going through the Scriptures from Genesis to Revelation, apply these rules to select passages that Trinitarians use in their attempt to show the deity of Messiah and the plurality of the one Elohim. These rules were used in Part One, but in Part Two they are spelled out.

PART TWO: OTHER VERSES

CHAPTER FIFTEEN

Rules of Interpretation

———∞∞∞———

> The natural man does not receive the *matters* of the Spirit of
> Elohim, for they are foolishness to him, and he is unable to know
> them, because they are spiritually discerned. (1Cor 2:14, TS)

THE SCRIPTURES ARE THE ONLY VALID SOURCE of authority
for understanding Scripture. No writing outside of Scripture, no
matter how revered or historical it may be, has any authority whatsoever
for explaining the meaning of Scripture. All such writings can do is give
an opinion; they are not inspired words from Elohim as the Scriptures
are. So we begin by establishing the Scriptures as the only authority.

When talking about a subject, there must be a base of authority, an
authority that is trustworthy. When a case is heard in court, one con-
sideration is the honesty of the witnesses. Suppose there were a witness
who knows everything and could not lie; whatever he said was true. And
suppose there were other witnesses who could lie and often did. If there
was a disagreement between the one and the others, which would you
believe? The obvious answer is, of course, the one who could not lie and
always told the truth. But let's add another ingredient. Suppose you did
not *like* what the one said, even though you knew he couldn't lie, and
you *did* like what the others said. Which would you believe?

*Human nature is to believe what you want to believe. Truth has nothing to
do with it.* But we want to think that what we believe is the truth, and so
we twist the truth to fit with the lie that we want to believe, and then we

believe the lie is the truth, and the truth is a lie. It happens all the time in life.

A classic example is the girl who falls in love with a bad man. Everyone tells her he is no good and he will ruin her life. But she loves him. She does not use her reason. She does not consider the evidence given her. She does not want the truth. She points out how kind he is to her, how he makes her feel loved and important. Because she loves him, she follows her emotions, not truth. And she gets angry with those who speak badly of him. She is deceived because she wants to be deceived. *Commitment to truth, regardless of personal pain and loss, is rare among us humans.* And so we are easily deceived.

> ... each of us has turned to his own way. ... All have sinned and fallen short of the majesty of Elohim. (Is 53:6; Ro 3:23)

What is deception? *Deception is believing something is true that is not true.* To the deceived person it seems true. It seems so true that it ought to be obvious to others that it is true, just like that girl in love with the bad man. If you love a doctrine and find out it is false, it is painful to give it up. Most will refuse to believe it is false. But if you love Yahuah more than any doctrine about him, then it is easy to give up false doctrine. Sadly, most Christians love their doctrines *about* God more than they love God. To them, their doctrine *is* God.

> For this reason God sends them a powerful delusion so that they will believe the lie and so that all will be condemned who have not believed the truth but have delighted in wickedness. (2Th 2:9-12, NIV)

There is someone who cannot lie and can only tell the truth. He is Elohim (Nu 23:19). He caused the Scriptures to be written (2Ti 3:16-17; 2Pe 1:21). The Scriptures alone are the word of Yahuah. The Scriptures alone are the written expression of the heart and mind of Yahuah for man. It alone is the truth. Whatever is not in the Scriptures is of man.

One of the basic doctrines that must be settled in our minds, hearts and practice is *the authority of Scripture.* That authority must be absolute.

The Scriptures, and the Scriptures alone, must be our only source of doctrine and practice. It, and it alone, is the written word of Yahuah Elohim. No other writing, creed, statement of faith or teaching must be allowed as having any authority in our lives whatsoever, no matter how revered, traditional or respected it may be, and no matter the church position of the person holding it. As with this book, all they can do is explain and try to give understanding of the Scriptures. What they teach, though, is according to what they believe. And if what they believe is wrong, then they are blind men leading the blind (Mt 15:4). Whatever these blind men teach, it can never replace the Scriptures or change it. The Scriptures must be used to teach all doctrine, and the Scriptures alone must be used to judge all doctrine, teaching, creeds, statements of faith and writings, not the other way around. But doing it the other way around happens all the time.

It is the habit of fallen man to change (or interpret) Scripture to fit what he wants to believe and what he wants to do. Fallen man resists change, and so makes excuses for his error and sin and rebellion against Yahuah, and interprets the Scriptures to justify his rebellion. Added to that, fallen man makes a religion of his rebellious beliefs and condemns those who disagree or teach differently. It is what the Jews did to Yahushua, and it is so today.

Let us look at what Yahuah has to say on the subject.

These [of Berea] were more fair-minded than those in Thessalonica, in that they received the word with all readiness, and searched the Scriptures daily *to find out* whether these things were so. (Ac 17:11, NKJ)

Every word of God is flawless; he is a shield to those who take refuge in him. Do not add to his words, or he will rebuke you and prove you a liar. (Pr 30:5-6, NIV)

Do not go beyond what is written. (1Cor 4:6, NIV)

Although translations differ, the truths are the same in every translation. However, the words that define the Trinity are not in the Scriptures.

Here are the Trinitarian words not in the Scriptures: "Trinity," "one-in-three," "three-in-one," "God the Son," "God the Holy Spirit," "three Persons of God," "God in Three Persons," "dual nature," "God-man." Trinitarians know these words are not in the Scriptures, yet they believe that the truth of them is. Why? Because they start with these words as though they are true, then interpret the Scriptures to agree with them, and ignore the verses that contradict them.

Not only does Yahuah warn against *adding*, he warns against *taking away* (Re 22:18-19). **The doctrine of the Trinity has taken away the truth that Yahuah is one and that he is the Father only. The doctrine of the "deity of Christ" has taken away the truth that Yahushua is a man, and man means man only.**

Read Isaiah 55:8-11. It shows how different our way of thinking is from the way of Yahuah. If we want to understand his word, then we must start thinking his way. If we interpret the Scriptures from our own natural understanding, we are guaranteed to be wrong. Every doctrine in the church is poisoned a little or a lot with man's natural thinking. None of it is pure. How do we get the thinking of Yahuah? *First, by getting to know him personally and loving him with all our heart, soul, mind and strength. Yahuah will only reveal his word to those who love him and want to obey him.* He hides it from all others. (See also 1Cor 2:9-16.) Only by the spirit of Yahuah can we know the thoughts of Yahuah and understand the Scriptures. It is impossible for the natural mind to understand.

Read John 10:1-16. In this passage Yahushua teaches that those who truly belong to him follow him because they know his voice. They recognize truth when they hear it, whether through writings or teaching, because it is the voice of their Shepherd, their Savior, their Sovereign, their Master.

In 1John 2:18-28 the apostle John writes the same thing. We need teaching, but we need to recognize if that word is from Yahuah or man. Recognizing his voice doesn't come quickly, just as getting to know Yahuah intimately doesn't come quickly. (See Heb 5:13-14.) But when we hear a little, and believe and obey that little, then he reveals more. The reverse is also true. If we don't believe and obey what he shows us from his word, then even what we have believed will be removed from us. (See the parable of the talents in Mt 25:14-30.)

Read Matthew 15:1-9 regarding traditions of man. Every tradition of man that is *not* taught directly from what Yahuah caused to be written in the Scriptures makes of none effect the word of Yahuah. Yahuah warns us not to join ourselves to things of Babylon, but rather to come out from among them (2Cor 6:14-18; Rev 18:4-5). This applies to everything in life, including religious doctrines and practices which do not please Yahuah.

Whatever displeases Yahuah, including man-made doctrines and practices in the church, is part of Babylon. Yahuah is going to judge Babylon and doesn't want any of his people in her when that happens. Read Psalm 1 and note the difference between those who follow only the word of Yahuah and those who don't.

I think the point is made: The Scriptures must be our only authority and to use any other writing or source as authority will lead to error. "But," someone might say, "there are so many interpretations of the Bible, how can we know which is the right one?" There is a way, a sure way. That's what this discussion is about.

If you have done any reading or listened to any teaching on the subject of the natures of Elohim and his son, you will have noticed that this book is far different from Christian tradition. So who am I to disagree? Well, point one, majority belief does not mean truth. (Nor, for that matter, does minority belief). And name-calling of a minority belief as being heresy and a cult (which they do against the teaching here) does nothing to establish truth. All it does is try to frighten people from examining the evidence for themselves and believing what the Scriptures actually say. They don't want you to believe what is written; they want you to believe what *they* say is the *meaning* of what is written. *They* want to be the authority, not the Scriptures.

I am not against them; I am for them. Many are sincere Christians wanting to follow Jesus and God, and they sincerely believe what they teach. But sincerity has nothing to do with truth. Muslim Jihadists are sincere when they butcher those who disagree with them. Hindu extremists are sincere when they slaughter Christians and Muslims. During the Reformation, the Roman Catholic Church was sincere when they massacred millions of Protestants and tortured thousands in the Inquisition, and Protestants were sincere when they killed Catholics. And I am sincere in writing this book, but that doesn't make what I write true.

However, there is a method for discovering what a writer means by what he writes, and that is using his own writings to explain what he means. As applied to Scripture, it means using Scripture to interpret Scripture. This is a general principle that applies to all writings, and it applies to all speaking. If I don't understand what you say, I ask you, and you explain. Even then I may not understand, but I haven't the right to say you mean something totally different from what you say, and if I do, I am accusing you of lying. In the case of Scripture, the author, Elohim, can't lie. (Then who is lying?) So let's look at some basic rules of understanding what someone says or writes.

What follows may seem a bit dry and technical. However, this is the foundation for understanding and will help you understand why certain conclusions are drawn. Without these rules you will always come up with "a house built on the sand" (Mt 7:24-27). So persevere. Let these rules become a part of your regular thinking apparatus. Some of these rules apply to all literature, and some specifically to the Scriptures.

1. All of Scripture is directly from Yahuah. It is perfect. (Although translations differ, the differences do not affect the whole teaching.) The Scriptures alone are the source for all true doctrine and practice. Yahuah warns us not to add or subtract from his word. The doctrine of the Trinity adds to the Scriptures. This rule condemns the doctrine of the Trinity as being a false doctrine. (2Ti 3:16-17; Pr 30:6; Rev 22:18-19; Ps 119:9-11; Is 66:2; 1Jn 2:5; 2Pe 1:20-21; Jn 6:63; 4:23-24.)

2. Use Scripture itself to interpret itself. Except for reference, do not use creeds or outside commentary. These are all writings of man. **Every true doctrine of the assembly of Messiah can be stated by using Scripture words only, and the wording of every true doctrine can be found in words of the Scriptures.** If the words needed to define a doctrine come *only* from outside the Scriptures, then that doctrine is false. This rule also condemns the doctrine of the Trinity.

3. The Scriptures have many writing styles. Some of it is to be taken literally, some of it figuratively, and all of it prophetically and spiritually. They are written to hide truth from unbelievers and from those who want to believe lies. The Scriptures have a purpose, and that purpose is to produce the bride of Messiah. (Mt 11:25; Pr 25:2; Eph 5:27; Rev 21.)

4. Get to know the Author. The more you know him and seek understanding from him, the more he will reveal. (1Cor 2:9-14; Is 55:8-11; Dt 4:29; Pr 8:17; Jer 29:13.)

5. The book of Yahuah is set-apart (holy). We should not revere it as an idol, but revere it as a manifestation of the will of Yahuah for us, a source of life and hope, and a source of warning and fear. We need to be very careful to discern what Yahuah is saying in it. The word of Yahuah will be accomplished, but only in those who submit themselves to him.

6. Recognize that if you use your own mind without help from Yahuah, you will always, always get it wrong. (Mt 13:10-17.) Yahuah has meanings hidden away in verses, here and there, that can only be known by direct revelation from him. The meanings will agree with scripture *and reason* once you see them, but you cannot see them on your own. (1Cor 2:14; Ro 8:6-8.)

7. Have pure motives. What is your reason for wanting to understand the Scriptures? Yahuah will hide its meaning from those with selfish motives. Your desire to understand the Scriptures must come from a heart that is desperate for the will of Yahuah to be done in your life and on earth just as it is in heaven (Mt 6:10). But, beware! It is easy to be deceived (Jer 17:9). So seek Yahuah for pure motives.

8. Be humble, have a contrite spirit, and tremble at the word of Yahuah. (Is 66:2.) You are not trying to understand an ordinary book; you are trying to understand what the set-apart one is wanting to communicate to you. Seek to be changed by what he says. Seek to love what he loves and hate what he hates. Let his word be a joy to you (Ps 119:16). Meditate on it day and night. Let it feed your spirit and soul (Ps 1).

9. Use reason. (Is 1:18.) Yahuah gave us a mind that can reason. Although we must depend on him for understanding, when he gives the understanding, it will fit with reason. It will not be a mystery which you must believe by faith and is contrary to logic and reason. This is another rule that condemns the doctrine of the Trinity, for that doctrine says it is "a mystery beyond reason." The more you understand Yahuah and his word, the more reasonable and more simple it gets.

10. Be guided by the general tenor (general teaching) of Scripture. The clear scriptures give a general truth that can be found throughout the whole of the Scriptures. When you get the *feel* of truth, you can sense what a meaning must be in a particular passage. This *feel of truth* only comes through personal communion with Yahuah, and grows the more you know him (Heb 5:12-14).

11. Let clear verses interpret unclear ones. Every basic truth in Scripture is stated clearly many times. If a passage seems unclear, use the clear ones to get the understanding. Trinitarians do it the other way around. They look for and use unclear verses to support their belief, then change the meaning of the clear verses to agree with their doctrine.

12. Let literal passages interpret figurative ones. This rule is an extension of the previous one. The Scriptures are full of figures of speech, especially the Gospel of John. A common one is *metaphor*. In this, something is said to be something else that has similar qualities. For example, when Yahushua said, *"I am the door of the sheep"* (Jn 10:7), he was using *metaphor*. Clearly Yahushua is not a literal sheep-pen door. Symbolic visions are also figurative and not to be taken literally. There are many other figures of speech besides these. One mark of a false doctrine is to use figurative passages to change the meanings of literal ones.

13. An agent or extension of an authority can be called that authority. This is another figure of speech. Several examples in the Hebrew of the Old Testament show this. In the Book of Judges the judges are sometimes called *elohim (strong one* or *strong ones),* a title which is usually translated "God." In Psalm 82:6 humans are also called *elohim.* Yahushua quoted this in John 10:34. Because the man Yahushua operated in the authority of Elohim, he can be called *elohim.*

14. Words must mean what they mean. Yahuah uses words according to their normal usage. If he has a special meaning in mind, he will give that special meaning. Otherwise, the standard dictionary definition is the one to follow. To change the meaning of a word to fit a doctrine is to both subtract from and add to the word of Yahuah (Pro 30:6; Rev. 22:18-19). Trinitarians change the meaning of words. They say for Yahuah "one" means more than one. And they say for Messiah "man" means something different from man.

15. The word "all" must be interpreted according to context. For example, when the Scriptures say, *"All have sinned,"* it means that is the general condition of man. But an exception is made for one man (Ro

3:23; Heb 4:15). Trinitarians disagree with this exception. They say the fact that he didn't sin is proof that he wasn't truly a human. And they say if he were truly human as we are, then he would be a sinner as we are.

16. Look at the passage in context. What is the setting of the verse? What is the purpose of the section, chapter and book? Some words have more than one meaning. Choose the meaning that fits general truth. Trinitarians don't do this. They choose a meaning that fits their doctrine, even though it is against the meaning of the context and against general truth.

17. Scripture cannot contradict itself. If a passage seems to contradict another passage, look for ways to harmonize it with the general tenor of truth. Sometimes Yahuah is wanting to show an aspect of the truth. Sometimes, however, the translators have followed their doctrinal bias instead of what Yahuah intended, or indeed what the Greek or Hebrew clearly says. Seek Yahuah on it. Sometimes you must keep that passage "on the back shelf," as it were, and then later Yahuah will give you understanding. Because Yahuah says over and over that he is one and his son is a man, no scripture can mean Yahuah is more than one and that his son is not human as all others are human.

18. Seek to understand the prophetic nature of the book.

> For whatever was written before was written for our instruction, that through endurance and encouragement of the Scriptures we might have the expectation." (Ro 15:4, TS)

This verse shows that the whole of the Old Testament is prophetic for us today. Some prophecies are clear, others are not. Some are hidden in a word or phrase that on the surface do not appear prophetic. Many prophecies have numerous fulfillments, with a final one far into the future. Prophecy has to do with the future (although it can also be for edification, encouragement and comfort, 1Cor 14:3),—from events near in time to those far away in time. But sometimes it is spoken as though it is happening at the moment and sometimes as though it already happened in the past. Yahuah knows all things, past, present and future. Since he sees things as having already happened, he can speak of the future in the past tense.

An example of the future-present is when Yahushua breathed on the disciples and said, *"Receive the spirit of set-apartness"* (Jn 20:22). He spoke as though it would happen right then. But that was not possible until after his ascension and exaltation (Jn 7:39).

Revelation 13:8 speaks of *"the Lamb that was slain from the creation of the world" (NIV)*. Does this mean that Yahushua died twice, once as the pre-existent "God the Son" before creation and a second time in the flesh? Believe it or not, some Trinitarians actually teach this! They do not understand the nature of prophecy. Hebrews 7:27 says he died once.

The Gospel of John has many examples of the present-past; that is, something happening in the present is spoken of as having happened in the past. Most of the verses that are used to "prove" that Yahushua existed before he was born are examples of this. E.g., *"Before Abraham came to be, I am (the one)"* (Jn 8:58). But these verses cannot be used to prove Yahushua preexisted, because it would contradict the clear passages that say Yahuah is one, the Father, and his son is a man.

19. Recognize that church tradition, even widely believed tradition, may be false. Just because a church says something is true doesn't make it true. You must evaluate tradition by what the Scriptures say. (Mt:1-9; Mk 7:1-13; Ac 17:11.)

20. Love Yahuah your Elohim and what he says more than you love your friends, family, pastor and assembly. Make a stand in your heart that you will believe the word of Yahuah and follow it regardless of what happens to you, your family, your assembly and others on account of it. In other words, be willing to be persecuted and misunderstood for believing and following what the Scriptures say (Mt 10:32-39; Php 1:29). Many people, when Yahuah opens their minds to see a truth, they believe it. But when persecution comes they turn away from it and no longer believe it. (Jer 29:31; 2Th 2:11.) Second Chronicles 18:18-22 has an example of Yahuah giving a lying spirit to those who don't want the truth. The parable of the soils speaks of receiving the truth with joy, then giving it up when persecution comes (Mt 13:20-21).

21. Learn to think "outside the box." That means, learn to think differently from what you are accustomed to thinking. Expand your territory of understanding (1Ch 4:10). Most people blindly follow what they grew up with, as though it is eternal truth. They think if it is in their head or in their church it must be true, and anything different must be false.

22. Use commentaries and Bible dictionaries for clarification. This was mentioned above. I have computer software with many Bible translations, commentaries and dictionaries. Writers of these outside resources have doctrinal biases, and these biases often show up in their writings. But they can be helpful in getting cultural and historical backgrounds. Sometimes they differ widely. What I find most useful, however, are Hebrew and Greek dictionaries.

Anyone involved in translating from one language to another knows that often there is not a word-for-word definition. A word in one language has many meanings, and maybe only one of those meanings corresponds to one of the many meanings of a word in another language. In other words, the meanings overlap, and the translator has the task of choosing which word to use. Sometimes there is no one word and the translator has to make a paraphrase to get the idea across.

Often, though, the translator's choice is based upon his Trinitarian bias. He is looking for verses to prove that Messiah existed as God before he was born. So he selects a word to support his bias, a choice which goes against clear verses, and thus misses the whole point.

If you follow these rules (or principles) with sincerity and honesty of heart, Yahuah will reveal the meaning of his word to you (Jn 8:31-32; Mt 7:21-27). All of these principles work together, each supporting the other. *To fail in even only one is to fail in all.*

What follows is more detail (with some repetition) regarding four of these rules.

1. Words must mean what they mean.

As an example, "one" means "one." It doesn't mean "three-in-one." It can *never* mean "three-in-one." It *has never* meant "three-in-one." In no language on earth does it mean or ever has meant "three-in-one." "One" always and only means a simple, absolute "one."

It has been argued: "What about a committee of three people? The committee is one, yet it is three people." It must be asked, however, is the committee itself one being made up of three people, as Trinitarians allege God is? No. The one committee is a simple, absolute one. It is not three committees in one, each person in the committee being a separate but equal committee. Did Yahuah ever say he is a committee? Some Trinitarians, however, believe that Elohim is a committee of three separate, individual Persons. This is polytheism, belief in more than one god or in many gods. It is also "tritheism: belief in three Gods; especially this is so in the doctrine that the three persons of the Trinity (Father, Son, and Holy Ghost) are three distinct Gods, each an independent center of consciousness and determination" (Webster's dictionary). But Yahuah says he is alone, he is one, he is the Father, and there is no other (1Cor 8:5-7).

What about this argument, "We are three people, yet we are one"? The answer is, "One what?" Always ask, "One what?" Are you three people in one person, or are you three people in agreement? Does Elohim say "we" when talking about himself?" The "one" is still a simple, absolute "one," not a three-in-one. When Yahuah says he is "one," does he mean he is an agreement?

Moses said to the children of Yisra'el: *"You have been shown it, to know that Yahuah himself is Elohim; there is no one beside him* [singular]. ... *"Hear, O Yisra'ël: Yahuah our Elohim, Yahuah is one!"* (Dt 4:35; 6:4). The chief god in the Egyptian religion was three gods in one. This idea about god was also believed by most ancient religions and is part of the Hindu belief today! Moses was telling the children of Yisra'el that in contrast to the pagan gods, Yahuah Elohim is one!

Here are a few other verses that say Yahuah says he is one.

"And this is everlasting life, that they should know you [Father], the only true Elohim...." (Jn 17:3)

For us there is one Elohim, the Father, from whom all came. (1Cor 8:6)

Elohim is one. (Gal 3:20)

One Elohim and Father of all. (Eph 4:6)

Most Trinitarians think of Yahuah as Three Gods, and they try to honor and pray to each in such a way as to give each of the Three equal honor.

When they use the word "God," they have to have in their mind which of the Three Gods they mean, or whether they mean all Three in a collective One.

Some Trinitarians try to use illustrations from nature to show that "one" can mean more than one. One example they use is the egg. "Look at the egg," they say. "It has a shell, the white, and a yolk. That's three, yet it is one egg." Let's look at this example more closely to see how foolish it is. The most common Trinitarian teaching is that each of the three Persons is equally *all* of Yahuah, yet each is different from the other. Is the shell *all* the egg? Is the white *all* the egg? Is the yolk *all* the egg? No! No! No! And what about the membrane between the shell and the white? Does that mean Yahuah is four-in-one? Anyway, Yahuah is not an egg. Pagans, however, did worship the egg as a fertility god and have made numerous idols of eggs. (This is the origin of the Easter egg.) The Vatican of the Roman Catholic Church has idol eggs carved everywhere.

Another Trinitarian argument is a married couple being called "one flesh" (Gen 2:24, quoted in Eph 5:31). However, it should be clear that neither person in the "one flesh" is the whole couple.

Trinitarians use many other things from nature to allegedly "show" that three-in-one is a natural part of creation in which Yahuah is trying to show his nature. This is pagan nature worship. Whether it is the sun with light, heat and rays, or a tree with root, trunk and branches, or a human with body, soul and spirit—it is all the same foolish argument. Each part of the whole is not the whole (as Trinitarianism alleges the one God is). All those examples are illustrations of three separate, individual Persons as being three separate Gods, as in the belief that "God is a committee of three." As said above, this is tritheism and polytheism, not monotheism.

To defend themselves, Trinitarians then say, "There is no example in nature that illustrates the Trinity. These examples only *hint* that God is a Trinity." Do they? No! A hint means nothing unless there is something real (in this case, Scripture verses) to hint about it. Since there is nothing, it can't hint at anything. Rather, what nature declares loudly is Elohim is one (Ps 19:1-3; Ro 1:20).

Yahushua also prayed that believers in him be one in the same way that he and the Father are one (Jn 17:21-23). One what? One in being, that we all together be God? Of course not!

It means one in purpose, one in mind. (Ac 4:32; 1Cor 1:10; 2Cor 13:11.) That's what Yahushua was and is with the Father, and that's what he prayed for us to be. In fact, this is the reason that was in the beginning; this is why we were created. This is what heaven is. This is what Adam and Eve were before they sinned. And this is why Yahushua came, that he be the means whereby we can regain that relationship. Only those who strive to be one with the Father and Yahushua as the Father and Yahushua are one can be in that kingdom (Php 3:12-14).

Those who don't strive to be in this oneness in this life can't be in the kingdom (2Pe 3:13; Rev 21:1). If a person hates loving and obeying Yahuah and his son in this life, it is impossible for him to go to heaven in the next life. If he did, he would hate it. Why? Because heaven is being one in purpose and heart with Yahuah so that he lives in you and shows himself to others through you and you see him in others. That's what being a believer is all about.

> "Your kingdom come, your will be done, as in heaven, so on earth." (Mt 6:10)

We have seen that one means one, and one means only. It is what the Scriptures teach. This is true monotheism. Monotheism means belief in one god. A monothe*ist* is one who believes in monothe*ism*. Monotheism is in contrast to polythe*ism* (belief in many gods) and trithe*ism* (belief in three gods, a limited form of polytheism).

Trinitarians say they believe in one God and not three gods, even though they believe this one God is made up of three equal and separate Persons, while each of the three is the whole. Therefore they call themselves monotheists (believers in one God).

But it is not the monotheism of Scripture. They call Jewish monotheism "absolute monotheism" and "strict monotheism," a monotheism in which one means one. Trinitarians, however, have changed the meaning of monotheism to mean something different from its true meaning; they have changed it to mean one-in three and three-in-one.

Judaism is the foundation of Christianity. The truths of the Old Testament didn't change when Yahushua came. Rather, he fulfilled those truths. One means a numerical one and never a three-in-one. For understanding any writing, including Scripture, words must mean what they mean.

Another word which must mean what it means is man. Hebrew uses the words *'adam* (ah-THAHM, th as in the) and *'iysh* (eesh) for man, and Greek uses *anthropos* and *anér* (an-AYR).

The dictionary defines "man" as an adult human male, any member of the human race, regardless of gender, and also humankind in general. This definition excludes god-men. The same is true with the Hebrew and Greek words.

Greek mythology is full of god-men. The myth of Hercules is one of them.[1] Although it is just a myth, this belief began in pagan cultural thinking when Cain started his own religion after Elohim rejected his offering.[2] An example of belief in god-men is when Paul healed a cripple in Lystra. As a result, the crowds called Barnabas Zeus (the high god) and Paul Hermes (his interpreter). Later, however, they stoned Paul and left him for dead (Ac 14:8-20).

Is Yahushua ever called a man? Yes. In fact, he is *only* referred to as a man and *never, not ever,* referred to as a god-man or as deity. It would be unthinkable in Jewish monotheism that any human could be deity or part deity. I use the word "deity" rather than "god," because the Hebrew and Greek words translated as "god" don't exclusively mean deity; the terms also include humans and angels.

When Peter spoke to the crowd during the Feast of Pentecost, he called Yahushua a man (Gk *anér*), referring to a specific male human (Ac 2:22). This same word is used for the lame man he healed at the temple gate (Ac 3:2). If he were speaking Hebrew (which is likely) then he would have used *'iysh*. They carry the same meaning as "a man" in English.

A common title for Yahushua is "the son of man" (Mt 8:20). The Greek word for man here is *anthropos*, meaning humankind. He is not just "a son," but "the son," the representative of the human race. The Hebrew would be *ben 'adam*, son of mankind.

---

1 http://www.perseus.tufts.edu/Herakles/bio.html

2 The development of all pagan religions, including Islam, can be traced through Babylon back to Cain. The reader can do his own research.

In contrast, Elohim *"is not a man* ('ish), *to lie; nor a son of man* (ben 'adam), *to change his mind"* (Num 23:19). In other words, Elohim is not a human being, nor a member of the human race. "Son of" means "bearing the nature of," either as a physical descendent, or having the nature of some quality, such as a son of peace.

In Matthew's genealogy Yahushua is called "son of David, son of Abraham" (Mt 1:1). The Greek has no article "the" with "son of," so, in line with Luke's genealogy, it should be translated as "a son of David, a son of Abraham." Luke's genealogy just has "of David" (Lk 3:31). Yahushua even said that the Scribes say (using Greek), *"that the Messiah is a son of David"* (Mk 12:35). As in the genealogies, the phrase isn't used as a title.

However, sick people used the title when they called out to him for healing, and so did the people use it in amazement when it happened (Mt 9:27; 12:23; 15:22; 20:30-3). They also used the title when he rode into Jerusalem (Mt 21:9,15). However, whether used as a title or not, what it does show is that the phrase "son of David" means he is a descendent of humans and therefore is a full human as all humans are. It doesn't show a god-man.

Another example of "words must mean what they mean" is the phrase "son of God."[3] When Trinitarians see the phase, their mind changes it to "God the Son." In every other situation, for example, they can see that "the son of Bill" does not mean "Bill the son." But when it comes to the son of God, their brain sees or hears "God the Son." To them, that is the meaning of "the son of God."

The same example applies to the phrase "the spirit of God." The Trinitarian's brain changes it to "God the Holy Spirit." Is there a difference in meaning between "God the Holy Spirit" and "the holy spirit of God"? Let us apply the grammar to humans. Is there a difference in meaning between "Bill the spirit," and "the spirit of Bill"? One identifies Bill as the spirit, the other identifies Bill has having a spirit. The two do not mean the same. John 4:24 says, *"Elohim is spirit,"* and most English translations do not capitalize "spirit" in this case. This means his nature is spirit.

---

3 Here I use "son of God" rather than "son of Elohim" because that is the common usage.

Man is more than spirit—he is body, soul and spirit. Yet we say of him, "He has a body, he has a soul, and he has a spirit." Who is the "he" that has these things. Is the "he" something different from the body, soul, or spirit that he has? No, of course not. As to his nature, man *is* a soul and spirit. Yet we say he *has* them. That is the nature of language. He both *is* and *has* the thing that he *is*. His body, however, is different from this. Man is not a body. He lives in his body like living in a house. The Scriptures call man's body a tent (2Cor 5:1-4; 2Pe 1:13). When his body dies, he leaves the body as a naked soul and spirit and gets another kind of body that can't die (1Cor 15:41-44). He still, however, is not his body.

When we apply this language to Yahuah, he is both spirit and has a spirit. The spirit he has is himself spoken of in a certain way, showing a certain kind of activity he is doing. Just as a man's spirit is himself and not a separate person of himself, so is it with Yahuah. His spirit is himself, and not a separate person of himself.

Does a man's spirit have a mind that thinks? Yes (1Cor 2:11). But a man's mind is not a separate mind of himself. He has only one mind. So it is with Elohim.

The phrase "God the Holy Spirit" was invented by man (Ro 3:4). Trinitarians use the phrase "God the Holy Spirit" to show a Third Person of a one-being-Elohim. It is not in the Scriptures, and there is no such thing. Think of the spirit of Yahuah in the same way you think of the spirit of a man. It always refers to a special activity or aspect of the one whose spirit it is. Use Scripture words only. These are the words of Yahuah. And then learn to use them in the way Yahuah (singular) intends them to be used.

This finishes this expanded rule of interpreting Scripture: Words must mean what they mean. This includes the rule: Don't change the meaning of words to justify your beliefs.

Rule 2. Use only words of Scripture to interpret Scripture.

Trinitarians bring in other words, words not found in Scripture, to explain what they believe. They say that although these words are not in Scripture, these words say what Scripture means. I ask, What kind of nonsense is this? Words of similar meaning can be used, but you can't just make up words that are contrary to the meaning of the writing. That is dishonest. In any other situation they would call it dishonest, but their belief in this doctrine is so strong that they do not see their own dishonesty. They may be sincere, but it is sincerity from deception. My prayer is that this book will help remove the shroud from their thinking so they can see the deception and believe what Scripture actually says.

Words that define the god-man and trinity doctrines are not only *not* in Scripture, they are *opposite* in meaning. It is like saying black is white and white is black. Here is a repeat of the major words: God the Son, dual nature, God became man, God-man, three-in-one, one-in-three, God the Holy Spirit, three Persons, and Trinity. None of these are in Scripture. They are all contrary to clear Scripture verses, and they are all from pagan mythology and philosophy. If you use Scripture words only, then there is no dual-nature or trinity doctrine because there are no words to define it. They have to use non-Scripture words, for there are none in Scripture. Without these words you have true monotheism.

Rule 3. Use clear verses to interpret unclear ones.

Unclear verses would include figures of speech and sayings according to Hebrew language culture, called Hebraisms. It also includes seeming contradictions.

Every fundamental truth in scripture is stated many times in clear language, and these clear verses form a general teaching that helps give understanding to all other verses in the Scriptures. If a verse or passage seems unclear or seems to contradict other verses, use the clear ones to get the understanding.

Here is an example. In John 17:3 Yahushua calls his Father "the *only* true God." Yet in 1 John 5:20, especially in the NIV, it seems to say that the *son* is called "the true God." In this verse the Greek grammar is not specific as to whether *"the true God"* refers to the Father or the son. By using proper rules of Scripture interpretation, however, we know it has to refer to the Father, for in John 17:3 Yahushua clearly said his Father is the only true God/Elohim, and the general teaching of scripture is that his son is a man. But even if the son *is* called "the true God," it is as the vice-regent of the Father, because of the rule that says an agent or extension of an authority can be called that authority. Also, because Yahushua is the exact image of the invisible Elohim, when we see him we see the true Elohim. (Jn 14:9; Col1:15; Heb 1:3)

Rule 4. Use literal passages to interpret figurative ones.

This is an extension of the previous rule. Do not take as literal what is intended to be figurative. For example, trees do not literally clap their hands. This is a figure of speech called "personification"; that is, something that is not a person is spoken of as though it is a person.

Another example is an attribute. In Proverbs 7-9 we see two attributes. The attribute of temptation is personified as a prostitute woman named Folly, and the attribute of the wisdom of Elohim is personified as a virtuous woman named Wisdom. Because Elohim used wisdom to create the world, many (not all) Trinitarians take this figure of speech as literal and say Wisdom is the Second Person of the Trinity, Jesus Christ. They understand that the woman Folly is a figure of speech, but they are blind regarding the woman Wisdom. They are blind because they are desperate to find something that shows Yahushua as preexisting, and so they *want* to be blind. In their blindness they are following Folly. It should be noted also that the word wisdom in Hebrew is feminine, not masculine.

These are the rules for interpreting the Scriptures, the foundation upon which this book is written. Throughout this book you have seen how these rules are applied.

By using the Scriptures as our *only* authority for doctrine and by following proper rules of interpreting Scriptures—the chief ones being "Let scripture interpret scripture" and "Words must mean what they mean"—we have seen that Yahuah Elohim is one, he is the Father only, his spirit is himself in some activity on behalf of man, and his special son Yahushua is a man only whom the Father elevated to the highest position of Master and Messiah. He is the pattern for the rest of us. Also we must keep in mind that the Hebrew words *Elohim* and *Adonai* and the Greek word *theos*, traditionally translated as "God" or "Lord," can also refer to humans. Every verse in the Scriptures must be interpreted to agree with these truths. These are the major clear truths by which to understand the meaning of unclear passages.

Trinitarians, because they use church tradition as their authority (as codified in certain creeds), do it the other way around. They start with their belief that Messiah is Elohim (traditionally called "deity of Christ") and that Yahuah Elohim is a trinity of three separate Persons (traditionally called "Trinity of God.") Then they hunt for anything that might hint at or give a suggestion of a plurality (more than one) in Elohim (traditionally called "God"). Once they can show a plurality, then they can support their belief that Messiah existed eternally as Elohim. Then they can interpret verses about Messiah to show his pre-existence. Their goal is to prove Yahuah Elohim is a trinity and that Yahushua is equally Yahuah Elohim as the Father is. Their goal is not truth (although they think it is), but to prove these doctrines.

What follows is summary from much study in the doctrine and history of its development.

Trinitarian scholars know that no verse says these doctrines. Further, they know that these doctrines didn't start coming into the church officially until 325 C.E. They believe God kept these "truths" hidden until all the monotheism of Judaism had been purged from the church. This "revelation" is so deep that God knew Moses and all the other prophets of the Old Covenant Scriptures wouldn't accept it. So he hid it in verses here and there without saying it clearly. God hid it in the New Testament as well, for the writers were too influenced by Judaism. They knew Yahushua was the Messiah, but their understanding was "clouded" by the "absolute" monotheism of the Jews. Yahushua, of course, "knew" he preexisted as the Second Person of God, but he couldn't say it openly. So he also hid his "true" identity in certain sayings. Paul and the other writers of the New Testament, however, didn't understand. So when the Third Person of the Trinity, God the Holy Spirit, inspired their writings, He also hid the "truth" in certain verses to be "revealed" later, until after the church had become thoroughly gentile. Then God inspired the Trinitarian creeds. The bishops who wrote the creeds were very corrupt in doctrine and life, but God worked through them anyway. "It is the truth that counts, not the character of the instruments of God," they say. It is these creeds that must be used to interpret the Scriptures. And once the Scriptures are interpreted according to the creeds, then they "prove" that the creeds are true.

This summary may sound crazy to you, but that is their thinking.

The "church" is deep into the "Deity of Christ" and its daughter doctrine, the Trinity. Every "Christian" book has some reference to them. These doctrines define "Christianity" as we know it. They are what *make*

"Christianity." Without them, they say, there is no "Christianity" and there is no salvation. Because of this indoctrination in the "church," many select verses are used to "prove" the trinity and the "deity" of Christ.

The goal of this book is to show that Yahuah Elohim is what Yahuah Elohim says he is (one) and that his special son is what he says his son is (a man). But there is a huge mountain of misinformation, false interpretation and deception to overcome. In the following chapters we will look at certain "unclear" verses. These are the verses that are used to allegedly "prove" the doctrine of the "Deity of Christ" (that he existed eternally as Yahuah Elohim before he was born as a man) and the doctrine of the Trinity (that the one Elohim [traditionally called "God"] is made up of Three Persons). We start with the Old Covenant Scriptures.

CHAPTER SIXTEEN

The Old Testament

———∞———

"Let Us" verses.

TRINITARIANS, IN AN EFFORT TO JUSTIFY THEIR doctrine, try to find evidence in the Old Testament that they can use to "prove," or at least "suggest" or "hint" that Elohim is a trinity. They say that when Elohim says "Us," it is the Three Persons of the one Elohim talking to themselves/himself. They say this phrase is *evidence* (although not proof) of the "truth" that Elohim, although he is one being, he is more than one Person (whatever that means). Three passages in particular they point to. They are Genesis 1:26; 11:7 and Isaiah 6:8. There is also a fourth passage in Genesis 18:1-17 that has three men, one talking to the others.

"Let us make man in our image," Genesis 1:26.

A principle of interpreting literature is to use ordinary rules of grammar. In all languages, when a person says "Let us," that one person is talking to others who are not himself. Therefore, our job as interpreters is to find who is (or are) the other person (or persons) Elohim is talking to.

When "one" is used as an adjective (as in "We are one"), we must always ask, "One what?" If there are three in the group saying "We are one," are they saying, "We are three persons in one being"? Or are they saying, "We are of one mind"? Whatever the thing is that they are *one* about, it is "a single thing or unit; not two or more."

Genesis 1:26 is a prophetic statement in which the Father is speaking to messengers (traditionally called angels) who were already in existence, but more specifically to his future special son, and also to those who will be conformed to his image, namely, the bride. It is prophecy.

There is a difference between Genesis 1:26 and 27. Verse 1:26 has the verb "make," Hebrew *asah*. This is a verb of process, such as having a piece of wood, and fashioning it into something for some use. Verse 1:27 has the verb "create," Hebrew *bara*. When Elohim created man, it was only the beginning. All of human history is the fashioning.

Trinitarians point to the word *elohim* as evidence that "God" is more than one. *Elohim* is a plural word. Because this word is plural in form, they say that this is evidence (although not proof) that Elohim is plural in nature. Hebrew grammar disagrees. *"Elohim* said, *'Let us make...'"* The verb "said" is singular. That makes *Elohim* singular, as singular as each individual person is singular. There is no hint of plural whatsoever in this. Let's look at verse 27.

> And Elohim created [singular verb] the man [singular noun] in his [singular pronoun] image [singular noun], in the image [singular noun] of Elohim he created [singular verb] him [singular pronoun]; male and female he created [singular verb] them [plural pronoun]" (Gen 1:27).

Trinitarians, in their attempt to find a plurality in Elohim in the Old Testament, use the nature of man as evidence of Elohim being triune. "Man has spirit, soul and body," they say; "that's three. Count them: spirit, soul, body." I ask, is this the image of Elohim? Are your spirit, soul and body three separate persons of you, the one being?

"Male and female are two, that shows plurality," they respond, "so at least the idea of plurality is there." I ask again, are the Persons of Elohim separate persons like a man and a woman are separate persons? Are these two persons in one person or being? In marriage they make one couple, but are they not still two separate individuals?

The fact is, Trinitarianism is tritheism—belief in three separate gods (a form of polytheism—belief in more than one god). Trinitarians pray to, relate to and worship three separate "Gods." Each of the three is

"God," making three "Gods." Count them: "God the Father," "God the Son," "God the Holy Spirit"; that's three. They give lip service by definition to "God" being one, but by one "God" they mean a "Godhead," or God-essence, or composite group, or committee of three "Gods." They do not mean one "God" in the dictionary meaning of the word "one."

"Let us go down," Genesis 11:6-7.

This is the second *"let us"* passage. Yahuah is speaking. The context is the Tower of Babel story in which Yahuah confused the languages so that different family groups would migrate away from each other and populate the earth instead of all being in one place. When they migrated, however, they all carried the same Babel religion with them. That's why all the ancient religions are similar, and in each the supreme "god" is a trinity.

To whom was Yahuah speaking when he said, *"Let us go down"*? Trinitarians claim he is talking to Persons of Himself, because no one else was there except Himself/Themselves. But who is doing the talking? If the name Yahuah refers to the whole Trinity, as many Trinitarians claim, and not to just the Father, as other Trinitarians teach, is it all three at the same time, so they are talking in unison?

But what if we take Yahuah as the name of the Father, who, the Scriptures say, is the only true Elohim? Ah! Everything is now clear. It is Elohim, the Father, talking to others who are not Elohim. How simple! How non-mysterious! Who could the others be? What about messengers? Elohim uses messengers to execute judgment.

The setting is a heavenly court scene. It is figurative. Sovereign of sovereigns Yahuah is on his throne surrounded by his messengers. On earth humans are rebelling against Elohim and wanting to make themselves to be Elohim. They are in unity because they all speak the same language, they have the same religion, they have a strong leader with Satan as their head, and all the people have given themselves over to demons to act in united rebellion against Elohim. The direction they are going has horrible consequences for mankind. Yahuah Elohim will not allow them to continue in united demonic strength. So he makes a court decision: *"Come, let us go..."*

"Who will go for us?" Isaiah 6:8.

This is a vision. It is figurative. Isaiah sees the Master in the temple and some winged seraphim. It is a court scene. The Master first asks, *"Whom do I send?"* singular. Then he asks *"Who would go for us?"* plural. To whom is the Master speaking? Was there anyone with him that he could be talking to? Yes, the seraphim. But the Master is also speaking on behalf of the whole nation of Yisra'el—indeed, on behalf of all mankind. He is looking for people to send. He is also speaking prophetically to us today. We are with Yahuah in his foreknowledge.

Three men, Genesis 18.

In this story three men appeared to Abraham to announce the destruction of Sodom and Gomorrah. Many Trinitarians say it is foolishness to use this passage as evidence of a plurality in "God." Nevertheless, some Trinitarians do use it.

To some Trinitarians this story is proof (or at least strong evidence) that Yahuah (singular) is three Persons (the three men). How strong is that "proof"? As the story unfolds, two of the men are messengers (i.e. angels), (vs. 19:1). These two messengers were sent to rescue Lot from Sodom and Gomorrah before Yahuah would destroy them. Messengers are not Elohim or Persons of Elohim.

What about Yahuah himself? He is left alone with Abraham, talking with him about the coming judgment. Yahuah is a singular being. This is a theophany (a manifestation of Elohim). Elohim is non-material, invisible spirit, but he can make himself appear as a human. Several times in the Old Testament Yahuah appears in physical form. The first was to Adam and Eve in the garden. The term "messenger of Yahuah (angel of the LORD)" may also refer to a manifestation of Yahuah.

Trinitarians interpret the theophanies of Elohim as evidence (if not proof) that Elohim would become a man. Of course, they start with the belief that Elohim did become a man, so they are using circular reasoning—using the conclusion as proof for the conclusion. When we use what Elohim says as our foundation, that Elohim is one, we come up with a different answer. Theophanies are a prophecy in type or illustration that Elohim would fully indwell a man. That man is Yahushua.

Conclusion

There are many other Old Testament passages Trinitarians use that they say support the idea that one means more than one, at least for Elohim. They say that although no one passage is proof, taken together, because there are so many, it adds up to considerable evidence.

Does it? Since each "proof" is zero, if you add all the zeros together, even if there were a million of them (which there aren't), you still have zero. Supporting evidence is no support at all if there is no hard proof to support. The only proof they have are words from creeds. There is nothing in Elohim's word. The hard proof from Elohim's word is that Elohim is one, the Father is the only true Elohim, and his son is a man. These are all words in the Scriptures. Proper rules of interpretation say: Use the Scriptures themselves to interpret themselves. Do not use outside commentary. Trinitarians can't do this.

CHAPTER SEVENTEEN

The Gospels and Acts

———∞∞∞———

IN MATTHEW, MARK, LUKE AND ACTS the humanity of Yahushua
the Messiah and the authority he has from the Father are clearly
shown. In the Gospels we read that Yahushua did miracles and forgave
sins. He did this because of the delegated authority the Father gave him.
That authority is also delegated to us. We also read that people called
him "Master" (Gk. *kurios,* traditionally in English, *"Lord"*). This was a
common title of respect, such as "sir" in English.

Blasphemy against the spirit, Matthew 12:31-32; Mark 3:30

Trinitarians use these verses to supposedly prove the personality of
the spirit of set-apartness, for, they say, "How can you blaspheme the Holy
Spirit unless he is a person?" Let's put that to reason. "To blaspheme"
means "to speak a word against," whether it is a person or a thing. In the
Matthew account Yahushua says speaking a word against the son of man,
referring to himself, shall be forgiven, but if spoken against the spirit it
shall not be forgiven, forever. The Mark account adds the reason. It was
because they said Messiah has an unclean spirit.

A thing to note in this incident is the lack of equality among the supposed three Persons of deity. If all three are separate but equal Persons,
as Trinitarians claim, then why can one be spoken against and be forgiven and not the other two? They answer that as to the Son, it is his
humanity that can be spoken against. But the passage doesn't say that.

It says that only if spoken against the spirit it cannot be forgiven. So that would mean that it is forgivable if spoken against the supposed deity of the Son (the Second Person), and also if spoken against the Father (the First Person).

What was the blasphemy? It was claiming that the miracles and casting out demons Yahushua was doing was from the devil and not from Elohim. They were attributing the power of Elohim to be the power of Satan. Remember, the term "spirit of set-apartness" refers to the Father himself doing actions on behalf of man. So to speak against the spirit is to speak against the Father. That is why the Father is not mentioned separately. The people Yahushua was addressing were monotheistic Jews. They knew that the term "spirit" referred to the Father.

Changing water to wine, John 2:1-11

The miracle of changing water to wine revealed the esteem of Yahushua; that is, the honor and anointing of the Father in him that he is the Messiah. This is prophetic of the last-day indwelling of the Father and son in the assembly. The best wine of Elohim's spirit is saved for last. Doing miracles is not evidence of being deity; it is only evidence that Elohim is working in that person.

Seeing the Father, John 6:46

"No one has seen the Father except he who is from Elohim—he has seen the Father."

We have already seen how Yahushua is from Yahuah. How did he see the Father? Not physically, because Yahuah is invisible spirit. How did Adam and Eve see Yahuah in the Garden of Eden? And how did Abraham see Yahuah? The three men who came to him were theophanies (spirit beings appearing in a physical form).

In John 5:37, Yahushua implied that he had heard the voice of Yahuah and seen his form. This is to be expected. Even Moses heard the voice of Yahuah and saw his form. In fact, Yahuah wants us to get so close to him that this is our experience as well. This is not a statement of pre-existence, but a statement of relationship of Yahuah Elohim in a man.

In John 8:56, how did Abraham see his day? He saw it by revelation from Yahuah Elohim. He saw it in the promise of Yahuah regarding his son Isaac, and he saw it again in the intervention of Yahuah to keep Abraham from killing his son as an offering. In the spirit he saw the fulfillment of this promise in the man Yahushua Messiah, and he rejoiced. Anyone who has had an experience with Yahuah of seeing a promise fulfilled in the future can identify with this rejoicing.

Father greater than all, John 10:29

Trinitarians claim that all Three Persons of the "Godhead" are equal. They make allowance for Yahushua during his human experience, and are blind to the verses that say the son is forever subject to the Father. But what about "God the Holy Spirit"? The truth is that the spirit of set-apartness is the spirit *of* the Father, an aspect or manifestation of the Father, and not a separate Person from the Father. The Father *is* greater than all, for he alone is Elohim, his spirit is himself for he is spirit, and his son is a human who never sinned and in whom the Father dwells fully.

Loved the praise of men, John 12:42-43

Still, even among the rulers many did believe in him, but because of the Pharisees they did not confess him, lest they should be put out of the congregation, for they loved the praise of men more than the praise of Elohim.

Like these Pharisees, many believers see the truths that Elohim is one and his son is a man, but they won't confess it because they know they will be rejected by their assembly and their friends. They love the praise of men more than the praise of Yahuah. The words of Yahushua in Matthew 10:37-38 apply to fellow assembly members as well as to family members.

"He who loves father or mother more than me is not worthy of me, and he who loves son or daughter more than me is not worthy of me. And he who does not take up his stake and follow after me is not worthy of me."

"My Father is greater than I." John 14:28

The Father is greater than the son because the Father is Elohim and his son is a man. All that Yahushua did was because of the Father in him. The oneness of man with Elohim doesn't make man Elohim. Man is the manifestation of Elohim; Elohim is the one doing the manifestation in cooperation with the man yielding himself to Elohim.

A man will judge, Acts 17:31

"[Elohim] has set a day on which he is going to judge the world in righteousness by a **man** whom he has appointed, having given proof of this to all by raising him from the dead."

Whose blood? Acts 20:28

"Therefore take heed to yourselves and to all the flock, among which the spirit of set-apartness has made you overseers to shepherd the assembly of Elohim which he has purchased with the blood of his own [son]."

How does the spirit of set-apartness make someone a pastor? By moving on him in his spirit and by prophecy. This is a manifestation of Yahuah. (Ac 14:23; 1Ti 4:14; 2Ti 1:6.) The terms "overseers" and "shepherds" refer to the same office of pastor. Note: Elohim (the Father) owns the assembly; he bought it by the blood of his sinless son.

Note Paul's warning in vs. 29. *"Savage wolves"* includes teachers of false doctrine.

"For I know this, that after my departure savage wolves shall come in among you, not sparing the flock. Also from among yourselves men shall arise, speaking distorted teachings, to draw away the taught ones after themselves. Therefore watch" (Ac 20:29-31. See Mt 7:15-23; 10:16, Lk 10:3 and Jn 10:12.)

CHAPTER EIGHTEEN

Romans to Ephesians

———∽∾∾∽———

THE LETTERS OF PAUL FOCUS ON HOW to live in Messiah. That life is in two aspects. One aspect is the nature of salvation; that is, what Elohim has done in the man Yahushua Messiah so that we may be reconciled to Elohim and be changed into Elohim's image. The other aspect is how that salvation will manifest in us as we let Elohim's spirit work in us. It is all done by the Father (the source) in his son (the word, the *logos*) (2Cor 5:17-21). The terms Elohim/ God/ *theos* and pronouns referring to him refer to the Father only, unless it is clearly stated in the verse or context to refer to the son. Although the Father is Elohim, the two terms have different emphases. *Father* emphasizes relationship, whereas Elohim emphasizes authority and power.

Trinitarians say God is three Persons and that God the Father is only one of the three. If they are right (which they aren't), then Paul and the other apostles should specify every time which of the Three they are referring to when they use the word *"God."* Even Trinitarians acknowledge, however, that the term *"God/theos"* always refers to the Father, unless context specifically dictates otherwise.

Romans

At the end of Part One we looked at the summary of Romans, showing that all the focus is upon the Father through the son. So we will skip to some select verses.

Spirit of Messiah, Romans 8:9

This verse shows two spirits. They are the "spirit of Elohim" and the "spirit of Messiah." This is the passage.

> But you are not in the flesh but in the spirit, if indeed the spirit of Elohim dwells in you. And if anyone does not have the spirit of Messiah, this one is not his.

These two phrases do not refer to the same spirit. The spirit of Elohim is Yahuah Elohim, whereas the spirit of Messiah is the spirit of a man. The word *spirit* has many meanings. One of those meanings is *attitude*. We can say of someone, "I like your spirit," meaning, your attitude. That meaning fits here.

The spirit of Messiah is the attitude that Messiah has toward serving Yahuah Elohim and desiring to manifest him. This spirit in a person shows that he belongs to Messiah, for he wants to conquer sin in his life and to promote Elohim's kingdom on earth. His whole life is focused on this. He is endeavoring with all that is within him to love Yahuah Elohim with all his heart, soul, mind and strength, and to love others as himself. Whoever does not have this spirit isn't a true believer. A day is coming when those who fully do this (by the help of Elohim's spirit) will be revealed to the world as the sons of Elohim, even as Yahushua was revealed to be *the* son of Elohim, the firstborn among many brothers. Elohim the Father is the source of it all. (Rom 8:9-29)

Over all, Romans 9:5

Who is over all in this verse? Is it the Father or is it the son? The Greek can be translated in either way. However, the one to choose is the one that agrees with the truth that Elohim is one, he is the Father only, and his son is a man whom he (Elohim the Father) placed over all.

1 Corinthians

What follows is a summary of 1 Corinthians similar to what we saw earlier in Romans. The focus is always on Elohim the Father acting through his son. It is by the will of Elohim that Paul became an apostle of the man Messiah. Messiah is the power of Elohim and the wisdom of Elohim. Elohim is the one who does the choosing. Because of Elohim we are in Messiah and Messiah becomes our wisdom—that is, our righteousness, set-apartness and redemption. (1Cor 1:1, 22, 27, 30.)

The spirit's power is Elohim's power in manifestation. Elohim is the one who reveals things by his spirit to our spirits so that we have the mind of Messiah. (1Cor 2:4-5, 10-16.)

Elohim is the one who does everything to make the kingdom grow. We are fellow workers of Elohim. We are the field of Elohim. We are the building of Elohim. Elohim is the one who gives the favor that enables anything to happen. Yahushua the Messiah, the son of Elohim, is the chief stone of the temple of Elohim, and we are all lesser stones. (1Cor 3:7-11.)

Elohim is the one who has given all authority to his son, the Messiah. (Except, of course, the son doesn't have authority over Elohim who gave the authority.) When this man has finished his work of building the kingdom of his Father—after he has destroyed all dominion, authority and power, including death—he will give the completed kingdom to his Father so that Elohim may have it all. They are Elohim's people. (1Cor 15:24-28; 16:10.)

One Elohim and one Master, 1 Corinthians 8:6

This verse shows that only the Father is the one Elohim. He is the creator and he is the one we live for. The man Yahushua is his agent, so when we live for him we are living for the Father. On account of Yahushua, Elohim created everything, and it is through faith in him that we live.

Rock was Messiah, 1 Corinthians 10:4

This verse says that the sons of Yisra'el drank from the spiritual Rock, and the Rock was Messiah. Did Messiah exist as a physical mobile rock keeping them company as they wandered through the desert? Some Trinitarians actually teach this! Remember the rule, "Do not take as literal what is figurative." Both the manna and the rock are types (or illustrations or shadows) of Yahushua Messiah. This is an example of typology being prophetic. Yahushua is the spiritual fulfillment of the manna and the rock. The truth is, the sons of Yisra'el ate physical manna, and they drank from physical water that came out of physical rocks.

Gifts of the Spirit, 1 Corinthians 12:4-11

And there are different kinds of manifestations of favor (gifts), but the same spirit. There are different kinds of services, but the same Master. And there are different kinds of workings, but it is the same Elohim who is working all in all. And to each one is given the manifestation of the spirit for profiting, … But one and the same spirit works all these, distributing to each one individually as he [the Master] intends. (1Cor 12:4-7,11)

In this passage we have "the Three." Trinitarians particularly love passages that have all three, for to them it is strong evidence of Three Persons in Elohim. Their doctrine has blinded them so they cannot see what Paul is saying.

The Greek for "gifts" is *charismata*, from which we get the word "charismatic." The root word is *charis*, which means favor. These are manifestations of Elohim's favor in power to help man. So a better translation than "gifts" is "manifestations of favor." That's why this word is connected to the spirit. What is the spirit of Elohim? By now the answer should be automatic: It is Elohim the Father (the only true Elohim) who is working by manifesting himself to mankind in some way. That's what the passage says.

"Master" refers to Yahushua Messiah, to whom the Father gave all authority. He is in charge of these manifestations of favor, both who gets them and how they are used.

When it says *"distributing to each ... as* he *intends,"* who or what is the "he"? The Greek has no pronoun. The verb *"intends"* is in the 3rd person singular (he, she, or it), so no pronoun is needed. Trinitarians like to have the "he" refer to the alleged "3rd Person of the Trinity," i.e. the Spirit. However, it is referring to the Master Yahushua, not the spirit. That is the context. (See Eph 4:7-8, 11.) Whenever you have a pronoun, you have to determine the antecedent, that is, the noun to which it refers. The closest noun it can refer to is "spirit." But the spirit is an "it" just as your spirit is an "it" and not a separate person that can decide anything. Elohim the Father is the one doing the working of the manifestation by his spirit. But Yahushua is the Master who has been given the authority for how to distribute.

2 Corinthians

First, the summary. Elohim, the Father of the Messiah, is the source of all comfort. Every difficulty we face is so that we will rely on Elohim. Sincerity and favor are from Elohim. Elohim is the one who makes us stand firm in Messiah. Elohim is the one who seals us with his spirit to show that he owns us. (2Cor 1:3,9,12, 21-22.)

Elohim is the one who leads us who are in Messiah in triumph. It is because we are in his son Messiah that we smell good to Elohim. (2Cor 2:14-16.)

The man Messiah in us that is seen by the world is like a letter written by Elohim's spirit on our hearts. Because of the man Messiah, we can be confident to approach Elohim. Elohim is the one who makes us able to minister. Elohim is the Master and is the spirit, giving us freedom and changing us from one esteem to a higher esteem. (2Cor 3:2-6, 16-18.)

The man Messiah is the image of Elohim. The light of Elohim in our hearts enables us to see his esteem in the face of his son, the Messiah. The power to share the good news and to endure persecution is from Elohim. (2Cor 4:4,6-7.)

Elohim is the one who is reconciling us to himself in his son Messiah. We are not reconciled to the man Messiah, but to Elohim. Because the man Messiah had no sin, Elohim made him to be a sin offering; and because of that we become the righteousness of Elohim. (2Cor 5:17-21.)

When we control our thoughts to agree with Messiah, then our thinking is no longer against Elohim. Elohim humbles us. The man Messiah lives by the power of Elohim. Our prayers are to Elohim. (Even when we pray to Yahushua, those prayers go to Elohim, for Yahushua is our intercessor.) He is Elohim of love. The love of Elohim makes effective the favor of his son, our Master Yahushua Messiah, and his spirit of set-apartness enables us to have fellowship. (2Cor 10:5; 12:21; 13:4,7,11,14.)

Messiah, Elohim, Spirit of set-apartness, 2 Corinthians 13:14

The favor of the Master Yahushua Messiah, and the love of Elohim, and the fellowship of the spirit of set-apartness be with all of you.

Does this show the Triune God as Trinitarians allege? Just because three are listed doesn't mean they are three Persons of one Elohim. Yahushua is the man who is the Master and Messiah of the favor to be given to us. The love of Elohim the Father, the only true Elohim, is the basis of everything. And our fellowship with one another and with the Father and Son is by the activity of his spirit.

Galatians

The emphasis of this letter is our freedom in Messiah to live set-apart lives by the power of the spirit in us rather than by the written letter of the law. Yahushua Messiah by the spirit of truth gives revelation. Elohim is the one who arranges our ministry, and he does it while we are yet in our mothers' wombs, and it is he who reveals his son in us. (Gal 1:12,15-16.)

In the man Messiah Yahushua we have freedom. Elohim justifies us (declares us innocent) when we have faith in this man, and thus we are able to live for Elohim. (Gal 2:4,16-21.)

The man Messiah became a curse by being hung on a tree, and thereby he redeemed us who are cursed because we have sinned, and he enabled us to receive the promise of the spirit. (Gal 3:13-14.)

Elohim is one (Gal 3:20), meaning one in nature. He is the Father. It is he who established the covenant of promise with Abraham and arranged its fulfillment in one of his descendants. That descendant is the man Messiah Yahushua, our mediator. The Old Covenant law with its physical regulations was a temporary covenant until the Messiah should come. Now that this man has come, the permanent covenant is based on faith in him. Through that faith we become sons of Elohim. Water immersion into the name of the man Yahushua Messiah is the act we do to confirm the covenant personally in our own lives. By this act we identify ourselves with this Messiah who died for us. Then, because we now belong to the man Messiah who is *the* seed, we also become seeds of Abraham and heirs of the promise. We are brothers together with this man, and his Elohim and Father becomes our Elohim and Father. (Gal 3:17-20, 23-29.)

Ephesians

The focus of this letter is the relationship of Messiah to the assembly by the power of Elohim. Because of the man Messiah, Elohim has blessed us with every spiritual blessing that is in Messiah. (Eph 1:3-14.)

Paul prays to the Elohim of our Master Yahushua Messiah, the esteemed Father. It is the power of Elohim that is working in us to know Elohim better and to know our inheritance. The power of Elohim that enables us to do this is like the power he used to raise his son Yahushua from the dead, to take him to heaven, and to give him all authority. That authority is for the assembly, the body of Messiah and the fullness of Messiah. (Eph 1:15-23.)

When we have faith in Messiah, we have a spiritual union with him. Thus we are a new creation of Elohim. Elohim is the one who gives us salvation, and we become his workmanship. The blood of the man Messiah enables anyone, whether Jew or Gentile, to come to the Father by his spirit, and we together become citizens of the kingdom of Elohim and members of his household. That household is a set-apart temple in the Master whereby Elohim may live by his spirit. It's foundation is men; they are the apostles and prophets, with the man Yahushua as the chief cornerstone. (Eph 2:4-22.)

It is through the assembly, the body of the man Messiah, that Elohim makes known his wisdom. Through faith in the man Messiah we may approach Elohim with freedom and confidence. (Eph 3:10-11.)

Paul prays to the Father that the power of his spirit may enable Messiah to live in our hearts by faith and that we may know the love of this man who died for us, so that we may be filled into the fullness of Elohim. Elohim is the one who does it. This one Elohim is the Father of all—he is over all and through all and in all. (Eph 3:14-21; 4:5.)

The exalted man Messiah gives gifts of offices to the assembly, his body. These gifts will operate until we all reach oneness in the faith, and in the experiential, accurate knowledge of the son of Elohim and become mature, attaining to the whole measure of the fullness of this man. We are created to be like Elohim in true righteousness and set-apartness of the truth. This is the bride that the man Messiah is coming for. (Eph 4:7-13, 22-24; 5:27.)

The armor we put on to protect ourselves from the devil is the armor of Elohim. (Eph 6:11-18.)

Messiah ascended, Ephesians. 4:4-8

This passage says Messiah ascended on high, but it quotes Psalm 68:18 which says Yahuah Elohim ascended on high. This is one of many examples in which what Elohim did in the Old Testament is attributed to Messiah in the New Testament. Elohim inspired both of these to be written. Is he confused? Not at all! It is an example of prophecy of the Messiah to come, in whom Elohim dwells fully, so that it is always the Father in him doing the works.

The Messiah and Elohim, (the Christ and God) (*ho christos kai theos*) **Ephesians 5:5**

In this verse we see a certain grammatical structure. *Christos* has the article "the," *theos* has no article, and the conjunction *kai* connects them.

Greek grammar has many rules, and it is alleged that the "Granville-Sharp Rule of Greek Grammar" is one of them. This rule states that if two nouns are of the same case ending and connected by *and* (Greek *kai*), and the first noun has an article (the) in front of it, but the second one has no article, then the two nouns refer to one and the same thing. This is the grammar in Ephesians 5:5 quoted above, and therefore some say this proves Messiah and Elohim (Christ and God) refer to the same being.

But there is more to the rule. If both of the nouns have articles, or if neither of the nouns has an article, then the two nouns may or may not refer to the same thing. Context must be used to discern whether they are the same thing or different. That is the so-called rule.

There is a big exception to this rule, however. If it is obvious that the two cannot be the same thing, then the rule doesn't apply. Because of this exception we have different translations.

The NIV has *"in the kingdom of Christ and God."* In a footnote it gives an alternate translation: *"in the kingdom of **the** Christ and God."* The NAS and the NKJV sidestep the problem by having: *"in the kingdom of Christ and God."* The NRS (New Revised Standard) has it a little different from the NIV, *"in the kingdom of Christ and **of** God."*

This subject is brought up because some teach that the grammatical construction of this phrase proves that Christ is God, and therefore deity. But it proves no such thing.

This arrangement of "article (noun) *kai* (noun)" appears frequently in the Greek Scriptures. One example translated into English is *"the God and Father of our Lord Jesus Christ."* This shows that *God* and *Father* are the same being or person, and Yahushua is another person. Another example is *"the Master and Savior of us."* The NIV translation reads *"our Lord and Savior."* *Master* and *Savior* both refer to the same person. In all of these cases it is obvious the two nouns refer to the same identity.

However, in Eph 5:5, if "Elohim" is referring to *Yahuah Elohim*, then the two are not the same in identity, for they are of totally different essence, one a man and the other Elohim, so a repeat of the article with *Elohim* is not necessary. It is one kingdom, and both Messiah and Elohim are ruling. Actually, the same principle is in English. If we say, "The lord and master of the house," we know they are the same person. But if we say, "The husband and wife," we know they are two separate things, yet it is the same grammatical structure.

However, as we have seen, the Messiah also has the title of "elohim." So the term could show the Messiah as also being "elohim," but not *the Elohim*. Indeed, Yahushua the Messiah is our Elohim (strong one). Why? Because of the authority of his Father given to him.

We will meet this rule again, and the attempt again to force it to make Messiah to be *Elohim.*

CHAPTER NINETEEN

Philippians to Titus

———∞∞∞———

Philippians

THE EMPHASIS OF THIS BOOK IS THE man Messiah who is the example of humility by submitting to suffering for the sake of the gospel (Php 1:29).

Emptied himself, Philippians 2:5-11

This passage of Scripture is used by Trinitarians to prove the deity of Yahushua. But, when using proper rules of Scripture interpretation, it shows no such thing. Rather, it portrays the attitude of Messiah Yahushua—his attitude as a man. What follows is a paraphrase to show the meaning of the passage.

Although having the visible form[1] of Elohim, both by creation and by being one with the Father, this man didn't try to be equal with Elohim. Instead, recognizing that he was a man only, he emptied himself of all desire for himself personally and took the visible form of a slave, and humbled himself by being obedient to death, even the shameful death of public torture and exposure. As a result, Elohim exalted him to the highest place of creation, the vice-regent of

---

1 The Greek for "form" is *morphe*. Meaning: 1) the form by which a person or thing strikes the vision 2) external appearance (Strong's database)

Elohim to be in charge of all the affairs of Elohim. And Elohim gave him the name[2] above all names, Yahushua (Yahuah is salvation), and ordained that every being in creation should bow in honor to him. When people confess that Yahushua Messiah is Master, it brings esteem to Elohim the Father. (Php 2:5-11, paraphrase)

Among theologians this passage is called the *kenosis,* from the Greek verb *ekenosen* in verse 7; it means *emptied.* The NIV has *"but made himself nothing."* The KJV has *"but made himself of no reputation."* Here are the first three verses in two Bible versions. Keep in mind that the trans-lators are Trinitarians. This is another example of theology affecting translation.

Let this mind be in you, which was also in Christ Jesus: Who, being in the form of God, thought it not robbery to be equal with God: But made himself of no reputation, and took upon him the form of a servant, and was made in the likeness of men" (Php 2:5-7, KJV).

Your attitude should be the same as that of Christ Jesus: Who, being in very nature God, did not consider equality with God some-thing to be grasped, but made himself nothing, taking the very nature of a servant, being made in human likeness. (Php 2:5-7, NIV).

Many Christians like to use The Living Bible (TLB), because of its clarity. The TLB is intended to be a paraphrase and not a translation. The purpose of a paraphrase is to make things clear, but it is an inter-pretation according to the author's theology, not a translation. Because the author is a Trinitarian, his paraphrase clearly reveals the Trinitarian interpretation of this passage.

Your attitude should be the kind that was shown us by Jesus Christ, who, though he was God, did not demand and cling to his

---

2 Yahushua had the name from eternity by the foreknowledge of Elohim and it was given to him at birth. But the full significance of the name could not be manifest until after his death for our sins and his promotion to the right-hand position of the Father.

rights as God, but laid aside his mighty power and glory, taking the disguise of a slave and becoming like men," (Php 2:5-7, TLB).

Note what it says, but do not be deceived by it. The TLB is saying Messiah was Elohim. He laid aside his prerogatives as Elohim (not his *nature* as Elohim), and *disguised* himself, becoming *like* men. In his thinking, Yahushua never really *became* a man, thus he never really *was* a man in the full sense of the meaning. Thus Yahushua is Elohim *disguised as a man*. Even though he "laid aside his mighty power and esteem," he still revealed it in the miracles he did.

In contrast, the paraphrase given earlier gives the true meaning of the passage, for it is based on the truths that the Father is the only Elohim, and his son is a man who had a beginning at his conception and birth. Paul wrote the passage not to show that Yahushua is Elohim, but to show the humility of this man that Elohim wants *us* to have.

We now continue in Philippians. It is Elohim who works out our salvation, for although he has given all authority to his son, nevertheless it is Elohim in his son doing the work. The man Messiah, being finite, has no personal power in himself. It always was, is now, and always will be Elohim in his son (and in us) doing the work. Nevertheless, as with the man Yahushua, we must yield our spirits to the spirit of Elohim for Elohim to work in us. (Php 2:12-13.)

To reach perfection, we must want *"to know him* [the man Messiah Yahushua], *and the power of his resurrection, and the fellowship of his sufferings, being conformed to his death."* We do this by bringing our requests before Elohim. It is Elohim who meets our needs according to his esteemed riches in his son Messiah Yahushua. (Php 3:10-14; 4:6, 19.)

Colossians

The focus of this letter is similar to that of the Gospel of John, for it shows the relationship of the man Messiah to Elohim on behalf of the assembly. Prayer is directed to Elohim that we may know his will and grow in the knowledge of him. Elohim is the one who has rescued us and brought us into the reign of his son. This son is the image of Elohim. All authority has been placed in his hands. (Col 1:9-20.)

The image of Elohim, Colossians 1:13-20

Colossians 1:13-20 is a parallel passage to John 1:1-18. What follows is the TS translation with some clarifications in [brackets]. It shows the truths that the Father is the true Elohim and his Son is a man.

[The Father] has delivered us from the authority of darkness and transferred us into the reign of the Son of His love, in whom we have redemption through His blood, the forgiveness of sins, who is the likeness of the invisible Elohim, the first-born of [over] all creation. Because in Him [on account of him] were created all that are in the heavens and that are on earth, visible and invisible, whether thrones or rulerships or principalities or authorities—all have been created through [on account of] Him and for Him. And He is before all [in position], and in Him all hold together. And He is the Head of the body, the assembly, who is the beginning, the firstborn from the dead, that He might become the One who is first in all. Because in Him all the completeness [of Yahuah Elohim] was well pleased to dwell, and through Him to completely restore to favour all unto Himself [the Father], whether on earth or in the heavens, having made peace through the blood of His stake."

The son of Elohim did not exist before he was born, but Elohim knew him by foreknowledge. Elohim knew he would be the word/ *logos* made flesh. So everything Elohim did in creation, and everything he has done since, is on account of what his son would be, and also for his son. It is on account of the son that Elohim holds all things together. He is the beginning of the new creation of Elohim and the firstborn of the resurrection. Elohim exalted him so that he is supreme in all of creation. Elohim had all his fullness dwell in his son, and because of that, all who turn to him can be reconciled to Elohim.

Messiah has power to operate that authority because in his body lives all the fullness of Elohim-essence.[3] When we are in Messiah, this fullness is ours as well. (Col 2:9-10.)

The authority that Elohim gave to the man Messiah over the works of darkness is given to us. Elohim is the one who has made us alive in Messiah through faith in Messiah and faith in the power of Elohim to do it. That faith is demonstrated when we identify ourselves with the man Messiah by being buried in water and coming up out of it. The power of Elohim removes our old nature and gives us a new one. We are dead to the old and alive to the new. (Col 2:11-15.) In everything we do, we do it in the name of the Master Yahushua, and we give thanks to Elohim the Father through him.

Fullness in Messiah, Colossians 2:8-9

Beware that no one capture you through philosophy and empty deception according to the tradition of men, according to the basic principles [demonic powers] of the world system, and not after Messiah. For in him [Messiah] dwells all the fullness of Elohim-essence bodily. (Col 2:8-9, brackets added)

Note: "Messiah" *(chrístos)* and "Elohim-essence" *(theótes)* are two separate things, the latter *in* the former. Is Messiah in himself? It shows that all that is possible for Elohim to be in a human is in Messiah. And Elohim gives it to all who are in Messiah, to the degree that each individually is able to receive. Compare this with Paul's prayer in Eph 3:19—"... *in order that you might be filled to all the completeness of Elohim" (TS).* The man Yahushua is the completeness of Yahuah. He is our pattern. We pray this is the pattern for all the rest of mankind.

---

3 The Greek for Elohim-essence is *theótes.* As "human-ness" is all that is involved in defining a human, so *theótes* is all that is involved in defining Elohim as Elohim. Everything of the infinite creator Elohim that is able to be in a finite created human was in the man Yahushua. Thus he is the word/*logos* of Elohim.

2 Thessalonians

Of Elohim and Messiah, 2 Thessalonians 1:12

[We pray this] so that the name of our Master Yahushua Messiah is esteemed in you, and you in him, according to the favor of **the** Elohim of us **and** master Yahushua Messiah.

This is another example of the Granville-Sharp rule of Greek grammar, a rule which proves nothing if the two items being mentioned cannot, by their very nature, be the same as to identity.

Timothy and Titus

Now to the King eternal, immortal, invisible, the only Elohim, be honor and esteem forever and ever. (1Ti 1:17)

For there is one Elohim and one mediator between Elohim and men, the man Yahushua Messiah. (1 Tim 2:5)

NOTE: Elohim the Father, the only Elohim, is the Sovereign eternal, immortal, invisible. Note also that he is the one Elohim, and his son, the man Messiah Yahushua (not deity) who gave himself as the ransom for all men, is the one mediator between Elohim and men. (1Ti 1:17; 2:5.)

Elohim will bring about the appearing of our master Yahushua Messiah. This Elohim is the blessed and only Ruler, the Sovereign of sovereigns and Master of masters. He alone is immortal and lives in unapproachable light. (1Ti 6:14-16.)

Revealed in flesh, 1 Timothy 3:16

And, beyond all question, the secret of reverence is great—who was **revealed in the flesh**, declared right in Spirit, was seen by messengers, was proclaimed among nations, was believed on in the world, was taken up in esteem. (1Ti 3:16, TS).

The KJV has "God *was* manifest *in the flesh.*" This verse obviously refers to Messiah. The oldest and best manuscripts do not have the word "*theos*/God" that the KJV and NKJV used for their translations. Because of that, some Trinitarians use this verse to make a case for Messiah to be Elohim. However, even if "*theos*/God" were the correct word, it would prove no such thing, for the agent can bear the title of the authority he represents.

The Elohim and Messiah, 1 Timothy 5:21; 2 Timothy 4:1; Titus 2:13

These are more examples of the irrelevant Granville-Sharp Rule. See Ephesians. 5:5.

CHAPTER TWENTY

Hebrews to Second Peter

———⟨∞∞⟩———

Hebrews

THE FOCUS OF THIS LETTER IS THE man Yahushua as the fulfillment of the animal offering system of the law. He qualifies to be this because he is the son of Elohim and Elohim made him into the perfect sin offering. Because he is that perfect human offering, Elohim made him our high priest forever. Thus he is able to make us perfect also.

Elohim appointed his son to be the heir of all things, and it is because of his son that Elohim made the universe. When we see the son, we see the radiance of the esteem of Elohim and exactly the way Elohim is as to his nature. Because of the authority Elohim gave this man, he is in charge of everything. After this man finished the work on the stake that our sins may be forgiven, Elohim gave him his present authority as his right-hand man. At that time this man became as much superior to the angels as the name that he inherited is superior to theirs. That name is Yahushua—*Yahuah is salvation.* He has this position because he is the son of Elohim. He became the son of Elohim as soon as he came into existence, but especially because of his three-and-a-half year ministry as Messiah culminating in his death and resurrection. It was a certain day in the history of man, although foreknown by Elohim for eternity. Elohim elevated his son so high, and the two are in such close union, that the son qualifies to be bowed down to and to be called elohim. This introduces the book of Hebrews. Everything in the letter has this as its foundation.

Here are two Old Testament prophecies used for the Son.

Elohim, your Elohim, Hebrews 1:8-9

In this passage we see both the son and Father called Elohim (Strong One, *theos,* God), but the son has the Father as his Elohim. This shows subordination, not equality. But, because the son represents the Father he also is called Elohim.

In the beginning, Master, Hebrews 1:10-12

> In the beginning, O Lord, you laid the foundations of the earth, and the heavens are the work of your hands. They will perish, but you remain; they will all wear out like a garment. You will roll them up like a robe; like a garment they will be changed. But you remain the same, and your years will never end." (Heb 1:10-12, NIV)

This passage is a quotation from Psalm 102:25-27 in which the reference is to Yahuah (vs. 22) and to El (vs. 24), not to *adon*/Master.

So, is this quotation in Hebrews saying that Yahushua Messiah is one and the same as Yahuah Elohim, as Trinitarians would have us believe? No, it cannot be. This is a prophecy of Yahuah Elohim being *in* Yahushua Messiah—Elohim in a man, and the high position of that man. Because of foreknowledge and the purpose of Elohim in creating man, and because his son is the key to everything happening on behalf of the rest of mankind, his son is involved with him in creation. Therefore, Psalm 102:25-27 applies to the son as well as to the Father—the Father and the son (Elohim and a man) are eternally one.

Hebrews chapter two gives more information about this man who is the son of Elohim. Elohim created man to be in charge of everything in creation, but made mankind a little lower than the angels. That includes his son as well, for he is like us in every way. Because his son suffered, tasting death for everyone, Elohim elevated him to his present position. Thus the son becomes the author of our salvation.

Chapters 3-10 show how the man Yahushua is greater than Moses, and therefore greater than the Old Testament law that Elohim gave to

Moses. Yahushua is our high priest who offered his own blood once for all. That priesthood is not from Aaron, who was under the law, but from Melchizedek, who was before the law. Melchizedek has no recorded genealogy, thus the priesthood is an eternal priesthood. The son, of course, did not historically enter that priesthood until the beginning of his ministry, at his immersion. But he had it in the foreknowledge of Elohim.

Regarding this priesthood position, Yahushua became high priest after the order of Melchizedek in his earthly ministry. He had to be a high priest in order to offer himself as the lamb offering, (Heb 7:27). The consecration to become high priest included bathing in water and anointing with oil, (Exo. 29; Lev. 8). The bathing in water was his immersion, the anointing with oil was the spirit of set-apartness coming on him in the form of a dove. The high priest is not permitted to tear his official clothes, (Lev. 10:6; 21:10). To do so would disqualify him from office. At the trial of Yahushua the high priest *did* tear his clothes, (Mt 26:65), thus disqualifying himself to offer the Passover lamb. Yahushua met all the requirements to be both the high priest after the order of Melchizedek, and to be the lamb without spot or blemish. Note: the clothes of Yahushua were not torn. After being raised from the dead and taken to heaven, Elohim appointed him priest forever after the order of Melchizedek.

The same yesterday, Hebrews 13:8

In what way is Yahushua Messiah *"the same yesterday and today and forever"*? The context is the faithfulness of Elohim, and this man fully represents Elohim, (Heb 1:3). The Father is in the son. So just as Elohim is faithful, so is his son. (See Heb 1:12; Mt 28:20; Ps 92:2,4; 102:27; Is 44:6; Mal 3:6; Jam 1:17; Rev 1:8.)

James

In the letter of James again we see everything is focused on the Father. In verse 1:1 James says he is a servant of Elohim and of the man the Master Yahushua Messiah. In verse 1:5, if a person lacks wisdom, he should ask Elohim. In verse 1:13 we learn that Elohim does not tempt anyone, for Elohim cannot be tempted by evil. But the son of Elohim was tempted, and the Scriptures say that Yahuah Elohim does not change. These truths are proof that the son is not Elohim as the Father is.

James 2:5 says it is Elohim who chooses. In verse 2:19 our belief is in *one* Elohim. Verse 4:4 says if we have friendship with the world it is hatred toward Elohim and becoming his enemy. According to verse 4:6 it is Elohim who opposes the proud but gives favor to the humble. And in verses 4:7-8, we are to submit ourselves to Elohim, and if we come near to him he will come near to us.

Again, note, all of this is in reference to the Father, the only true Elohim, and on the basis of what Yahushua Messiah did for us.

Peter

Spirit concerning Messiah in them, 1 Peter 1:11-13

This passage speaks of the spirit **concerning** Messiah that was in the prophets. Trinitarian scholars translate it *"Spirit of Christ."*

The Greek has no preposition for *of*. The idea is carried in the case ending of the noun or pronoun. In this passage *spirit* is in the nominative case, showing subject, and *Messiah* is in the genitive case, showing several possibilities of relationship to the subject. In Romans 8:9 the phrase *"spirit of Messiah"* is a proper translation, for it is talking about the attitude the man Messiah has toward Elohim. In this verse, however, the translation that fits the context is *"spirit concerning Messiah,"* because Messiah was not yet in existence. It shows the spirit of set-apartness giving revelation to the prophets regarding the human Messiah to come. What Peter wrote in his second letter supports this translation. *"For prophecy never came by the will of man, but men of Elohim spoke, being moved by the spirit of set-apartness"* (2Pe 1:21).

"Of our God and Savior Jesus Christ," 2 Peter 1:1

Verse 1 is in the pattern of the (so-called) Granville-Sharp Rule of Greek Grammar in which the two nouns (God and Savior) refer to the same identity, but only if the two can be the same identity. But, as we have seen many times, they cannot have the same identity because one is infinite and the other finite.

Verse 2 has an article with both nouns, although the articles aren't seen in our English translations: *"of God and of Jesus our Lord."* This verse, because of the two articles, shows separation as to identity.

CHAPTER TWENTY ONE

First John to Revelation

—◦◦◦—

Gnosticism

A T THE TIME OF YAHUSHUA AND THE early assembly there were many "mystery religions." A mystery religion means an initiate must go through certain rites to be saved. These rites are secret from outsiders. An example of a current day mystery religion is Mormonism. They have all sorts of secret rites to follow to be saved. A popular one at the time of John was called *Gnosticism*. The word means "belief in knowledge for salvation." This was a special mystery knowledge.

> **Gnosticism**, n. an occult salvational system, heterodox and syncretistic, stressing *gnosis* as essential, viewing matter as evil, and variously combining ideas derived esp. from mythology, ancient Greek philosophy, ancient religions, and, eventually, from Christianity. (Webster's New World Dictionary)

In Gnostic belief, spirit is good and physical matter is evil. If this is the case, how could Elohim, a spirit, create the physical world? He did it through *emanations*. He emanated a spirit, and that spirit another, and that spirit another, and on and on, each less than the previous, and thus each less good than the previous, until finally there was an *emanation* far enough below and less good than the first one, and thus with enough evil that he could create the world. This *emanation,* said the Gnostics,

149

is the God of the Old Covenant. The secret knowledge is to know the names of all these *emanations*.

When Yahushua came the Gnostics added him to the *emanations,* placing him high on the list, far above Elohim of the Old Covenant. They said he was good, therefore he didn't have a body of flesh. The body that you saw was not real; it was an apparition. There was no real birth, no real temptation, no real death, and no real resurrection. He did not really die for us, nor shed any real blood. It was apparition only. Salvation is by knowing this secret knowledge about Yahushua.

This may sound foolish to our ears, but it was seriously believed by thousands, and many believers were being led astray to believe it. John's writings particularly address this problem, and it is stated specifically in 2 John 7.

> Many deceivers, who do not acknowledge Jesus Christ as coming in the flesh, have gone out into the world. Any such person is the deceiver and the antichrist. (2Jn 7, NIV)

If you do not believe in a real, human physical Yahushua then you cannot be saved.

Is Gnosticism in the church today? Yes. A form of it is. Any doctrine which denies the real humanity of Yahushua—a humanity the same as all other humans, a humanity that is human only—is a form of Gnosticism. The doctrine of the Trinity is an example, along with any other doctrine that believes in the "deity" of Messiah. The Athanasian creed says you must believe this "mystery" to be saved. Trinitarians are not fully Gnostic, for they allege belief that Yahushua was a real human with flesh and his death and resurrection are real, but the kind of human they say he is is not like any other human, for he is a God-man.

1 John

From the beginning, 1 John 1:1-2

> What was from the beginning, what we have heard, what we have seen with our eyes, what we have looked upon, and our hands have

handled, concerning the word of the life: And the life was manifested, and we have seen, and bear witness, and announce to you that everlasting life which was with the Father and was manifested to us." (1Jn 1:1-2)

This first letter of John has the same message of the relationship of the Father being in the son as does his Gospel. The first two verses echo the first eighteen verses of John 1. His Gospel begins with the words, *"In the beginning was the Word."* This letter begins with: *"What was from the beginning,"* (the Greek has no article), and identifies it as *"the word of the life."* The Greek has an article with both these nouns, thus emphasizing a particular *the word* and a particular *the life.*

As we saw earlier, the *word/logos* is the nature, soul, character and desire of Elohim the Father—his moral essence, as it were. It is also the law of righteousness in Yahuah. But it was made flesh in his son Yahushua Messiah. This is how the apostles were able to touch and handle it. It is in this *word/logos* made flesh that we have the very *life* of Elohim. Our fellowship is with both the son and the Father (v. 3), for the two are one. John wants us to share in that fellowship also.

What kind of fellowship is John talking about? Is it a gathering at a "church" social? Is it a gathering at a worship service? Is it cooperating in assembly and mission activities? No, it is none of these. It is the fellowship we saw earlier in John 17:21-23. John is writing this letter to talk about this fellowship and how we get it. The letter is rich in spiritual truth, but all that can be given here are a few highlights, particularly as they relate to the Father (deity) being in the son (humanity) so that we can have that same relationship.

Yahushua our Counselor, 1 John 2:1

We have an intercessor with the Father, Yahushua Messiah.

"Intercessor" is translated from the Greek *parakleton,* or Counselor. It is the same word used to describe the spirit of set-apartness. Praise Elohim, we have someone to turn to when we sin. Messiah not only speaks for us as our mediator, but he helps us overcome sin so we can become like him and have fellowship with him.

Acknowledge the Son, 1 John 2:22-23

Who is the liar, except the one denying that Yahushua is the Messiah? This is the anti-Messiah, the one denying the Father and the son. **No one denying the son has the Father**. The one confessing the son has the Father as well. (1Jn 2:22-23. See also 1Jn 4:15.)

These passages affirm the relationship between the Father and son and reinforce the truth that Yahushua is the only way to the Father. "Messiah" is a title of office. It means the man whom Elohim has anointed to rule mankind on his behalf. It is a title of humanity, not "deity." Note: To deny the humanity of Yahushua is to deny the Father and the son. The doctrine of the Trinity affirms the humanity of the son, but the humanity it affirms is in words only, for he is not a human as all other humans are human, for in that doctrine he is a God-man, not a man.

Destroy the devil's work, 1 John 3:8

The one doing sin is of the devil, because the devil has sinned from the beginning. For this purpose the son of Elohim was manifested: to destroy the works of the devil. (1Jn 3:8)

Elohim used this man to defeat the devil, and he wants us to join him. The bride will do this in the male-son ministry. (Rev 12:5,11.) It should be our desire to do this wholeheartedly, both in our lives and in ministering to others. (See 1Jn 3:2; 1Cor 13:12; Rev 12:11.)

The focus of the Gospel of John is the oneness of the Father and son. Belief in the son, therefore, brings life. The focus of First John is the oneness of the sons of Elohim with the Father and son and how that life operates in the believer.

Laid down his life, 1 John 3:16

Hereby perceive we the love of God, because he laid down his life for us:" (1Jn 3:16, KJV).[1]

---

1 No manuscript of the Greek NT has "of God." The KJV added it.

Elohim did not lay aside his life. Impossible! It was a man who laid down his life.

Three that bear record, 1 John 5:7-8

> For there are three that bear record *in heaven, the Father, the Word, and the Holy Ghost: and these three are one. And there are three that bear witness in earth*, the Spirit, and the water, and the blood: and these three agree in one" (1Jn 5:7-8, KJV).

Some Trinitarians like this passage, for it says the three are one. Note, this is the King James Version. The words in italics, however, are not genuine. It was added to the Greek text by the Roman Catholic Church around the time of the Reformation. The KJV translators thought it was authentic, so they included it in their translation. Most newer translations, also done by Trinitarians, omit these words.

Nevertheless, even if the words were authentic, would they prove the Trinity? Would they be able to cancel and overturn and change the truth that Elohim is one? Not at all! The Father is Elohim, the word is his heart-desire for a people to be like him, and his spirit of set-apartness is himself in a special activity on behalf of man. Of course they are one, but not three Persons. Leaving out the words in italics in the KJV, in what way do the spirit, water and blood agree? Are these a trinity of Persons? This is the passage with verse 6 added.

> This is the one that came by water and blood: Yahushua Messiah, not only by water, but by water and blood. And it is the spirit which bears witness, because the spirit is the truth. Because there are three which bear witness: the Spirit, and the water, and the blood. And the three are in agreement. (1Jn 5:6-8)

Water and blood are not persons. They have to do with a witness about Yahushua, specifically his humanity. One interpretation of *"water and blood"* comes from John 19:34 — *"But one of the soldiers pierced his side with a spear, and instantly blood and water came out."* The water and blood have to do with Yahushua, as our high priest, offering himself as the slaughter offering for our sins. In the Old Covenant offering system, of which Yahushua is the fulfillment, both water and blood are involved. It was a man who died. Elohim cannot die.

Throughout his ministry Yahushua had the spirit without limit, and he spoke only what the Father gave him. What Yahushua said and what he did are in agreement. And the spirit testified of the truth to all who had ears to hear the truth. That same spirit is speaking today. *"He who has an ear, let him hear what the spirit says to the assemblies"* (Rev. 2:29).

2 John

The two are one, 2 John vs. 3

> Favor, compassion, peace be with you from Elohim the Father, and from the Master Yahushua Messiah, the son of the Father, in truth and love.

This short letter carries the same truths as the rest of the writings of John. Favor, compassion and peace come from both Elohim the Father and from his son. The two are one.

Book of Revelation

This figurative and symbolic book of John shows the Messiah in the last days of the assembly and in the new heaven and the new earth. He is the triumphant Messiah, yet he is not the Messiah alone. The Father and son are in each other—the two are one. The Father is Elohim, and the son is the word/*logos* of Elohim, now exalted with all authority from the Father.

Father and Son, Revelation 1:4-8

Here are a few verses regarding the relationship of the Father and Son. In verses 4 and 5 we have favor and peace coming from 1) *"him who is, and who was, and who is to come"* (the Father), from 2) *"the seven spirits before his throne,"* (the seven-fold aspect of the Father, see Isa 11:2), and from 3) *"Yahushua Messiah, who is the faithful witness, the firstborn from the dead, and the ruler of the kings of the earth."*

This is not three Persons of a God-essence, each being all of the God-essence yet different from each other. In this greeting the Father by his spirit and through his son is giving favor and peace to the assemblies of Messiah, particularly to these seven assemblies which represent all the assembly throughout history.

Verse 6 tells us that Messiah made us to be a kingdom of priests to serve his Elohim and Father. Always Messiah does everything to honor and benefit his Father.

Vision of Messiah, Revelation 1:17-18

John had a vision of Messiah in blazing authority to bring judgment. In that vision Yahushua said he is *"the First and the Last,"* showing his union with his Father.

In a vision you know things by revelation as Elohim gives it, not by natural reasoning of appearances. What Yahushua looks like in the vision is not what the risen Messiah with a new body looks like. It is a symbolic vision of the authority of Messiah, particularly at the end of the age, called the Day of Yahuah (Day of the LORD), when Messiah will judge the assembly and the nations.

The Lion and Root, Revelation 5:5

Revelation 4 and 5 describe a throne-room scene. In this scene we see the relationship between Elohim the Father and his son as one. Chapter 5 is about the son. Verse 5 shows this relationship. Yahushua is called *"the lion of the tribe of Judah,"* showing humanity, and *"the root of David,"* showing his union with the Father who is the source of David.

The New Jerusalem, Revelation 21

In the bride of Messiah we see the completion of the indwelling of Elohim in man: Elohim *in* the Lamb *in* the bride. She is described as the

New Jerusalem in Revelation 21:1 – 22:5. The most important part of the description for our purposes is as follows. Words in brackets are added commentary.

> Rev. 21:21-23. And the street of the city [the bride] was clean gold *[nature of Elohim]*, like transparent glass *[Elohim is clearly seen in her]*. And I saw no Dwelling Place in her *[the bride]*, for Yahuah El Shaddai *[the Father]* is her Dwelling Place, and the Lamb *[the son]*. And the city *[the bride]* had no need of the sun, nor of the moon, to shine in her, for the esteem of Elohim *[the Father]* lightened it, and the Lamb is its lamp.

> Rev. 22:1-5. And he showed me a river of water of life, clear as crystal, coming from the throne of Elohim and of the Lamb *[one throne, the Father in the son, with eternal life flowing from them]*. In the middle of its *[the bride's]* street, and on either side of the river, was the tree of life, which bore twelve fruits, each tree yielding its fruit every month. And the leaves of the tree *[in the bride]* were for the healing of the nations *[the bride in another figure]*. And no longer shall there be any curse, and the throne of Elohim and of the Lamb *[one throne, the Father in the son]* shall be in it *[the bride]*, and his servants *[the bride in yet another figure]* shall serve him *[the Father in the son]*. And they shall see his face *[the Father in the son]*, and his Name *[Yahushua]* shall be upon their foreheads. And night shall be no more, and they shall have no need of a lamp or the light of the sun, because Yahuah Elohim *[the Father in the son]* shall give them light. And they shall reign forever and ever.

The chief focus of this book is the nature of Elohim the Father, and Messiah (the son of Elohim, a man), and their relationship with each other. Along with that focus the bride of Messiah is mentioned as a fulfillment of that relationship in mankind.

This symbolic picture of the New Jerusalem is the fulfillment of the prayer of Yahushua in John 17:21-23. These called-out-ones have become one with the Father and son in the same way the Father and son are one. Together—Yahuah in Messiah in the bride—they are one. This is the purpose of creation: *"Let us make man in our image, according to our likeness"* (Gen 1:2).

I am the beginning and end, Revelation 22:12-16

These final words of Yahushua, the last in John's vision and the last in the Scriptures, again show the union of the Father and son, the two in each other so they are viewed as one being. This kind of union is what Elohim wants for us with each other and with them. Those who achieve this union are the bride.

> "I am the Alpha and the Omega, the First and the Last, the Beginning and the End." ... "I am the Root and the Offspring of David, and the bright Morning Star." (Rev 22:13,16, NIV)

Conclusion

What John saw and experienced in the relationship between the Father and son, Elohim wants us also to see and experience. There is much more to be said about this relationship, but this description is a beginning. The son is the word/*logos* made flesh, for in him Elohim, the Father, lived fully. He possessed all the essence of the nature and character of Elohim. He shared the soul of Elohim. This is what he wants for us. The bride will achieve this, for those who comprise her as a body seek this relationship with all their heart. It is the fulfillment of the greatest commandment, to love Yahuah your Elohim with all your heart, with all your soul, with all your mind, and with all your strength.

CHAPTER TWENTY TWO

Conclusion

———∞∞∞———

VERY BRIEFLY WE HAVE EXAMINED THE ENTIRE Scriptures and have seen that the witness is the same throughout: Elohim the Father is the only true Elohim, his spirit is himself in some activity in and on behalf of man, and his son is a man in whom Elohim lived fully so that the two are one. Because of this union he is called the word of Elohim. To see the son is to see Elohim, for the son is the soul, heart, purpose, plan and reason (word/*logos*) of Elohim made flesh, and thus he can be called Elohim. This is the meaning of indwelling in the Scriptures, namely, Elohim *in* flesh.

The Elohim we serve is one, and his son Yahushua Messiah is a man. It is important to believe this, for only then is it possible to understand how Elohim wants to be in us. Because of their belief in the deity of Messiah they see Messiah's deity everywhere, even though it is not anywhere. An example is the phrase "God *in* Christ." Their eyes read the words, but their brain says, "God *is* Christ." It is similar to what was mentioned in an earlier chapter, that when Trinitarians physically see and hear the phrase "Son of God," their brain changes it to mean "God the Son."

To be fair to the Trinitarians, regarding the phrase "God in Christ," they recognize that God the Father is in Messiah, and the two are separate as far as identity is concerned. But they have to do mental gymnastics to do so. To them, *Christ* means "God the Son." So "God in Christ" means "God in God." The two are separate Persons, but each is the whole.

The average Trinitarian in the assembly does not understand what he believes, and usually doesn't want to. He just believes the words and is content with that and goes on his way without paying any attention to the implications of what he is believing. Their pastors and Bible teachers keep hammering the doctrine into them, with "Scripture proof" and "logic," and with the horrors of being a heretic for non-belief. So they blindly follow. They want to keep safe from false doctrine and they want to please God.

Throughout this book belief in the deity of Christ and belief that God is a trinity were shown in sharp contrast to what the Scriptures really teach. This was done to help the follower of truth cleanse such thinking from his mind. *"If you stay in my word, you are truly my disciples, and you shall know the truth, and the truth shall make you free,"* said Yahushua (Jn 8:31-32). It is my desire to help the assembly be free. For this reason I am bringing the truth.

Does it really matter that much? one may ask. Consider this: The doctrine of the Deity of Christ is an idol, and so also is the doctrine of the Trinity. Belief in them is idolatry, and Elohim will soon judge the church because of it, along with other sins, *"Because it is time for judgment to begin from the house of Elohim"* (1Pe 4:17. See also 1Cor 3:10-15).

The truth of who Elohim is, and what his nature is, is more than about judgment. Without the truth one cannot know the nature of that to which Elohim is calling him. Yahuah Elohim wants union with man so that man can be a manifestation of his love, beauty and set-apartness. That is the purpose of creation. But it can only happen as man is made in his image and likeness. The first man to be fully made in his image was his son Yahushua. He is our example. Because Yahushua yielded fully to and cooperated wholeheartedly with that making, Yahuah Elohim inhabited him fully, and the two became one. That is the union Yahuah wants with us. That is the union of the bride with one another and with the Father and son. Yahuah wants to be in us the same way that he was in his son. That was the prayer of Yahushua in John 17:21-23..

As this book has shown with abundant evidence, Elohim is one: he is the Father only, his Spirit is himself (the term used to show some activity of Elohim regarding humans), and he has a unique son, the man Yahushua Messiah.

This is our heritage from Judaism. It is what the prophets of the Old Covenant Scriptures believed and taught, it is what Yahushua believed and taught, and it is what the early assembly believed and taught. This is the Scripture meaning of "monotheism." Only this is true monotheism.

SUPPLEMENT ONE

The Idol of Jealousy

And he said to me, "Son of man, lift your eyes toward the north." And I lifted my eyes northward, and north of the altar gate I saw this image of jealousy in the entrance. (Eze 8:5)

In this Supplement we will take a brief look at the history regarding the Catholic church, what the Catholic church is, how the doctrine of the deity of Christ and its daughter doctrine the Trinity came into the church, some creeds of the Catholic church, why these creeds are not scriptural, and what their spiritual source is.

Catholic church defined

The Catholic church has three branches. The largest is the Roman Catholic Church (RCC). This is the Roman branch of the Catholic church, ruled by one head, called the Pope. Normally when people say *Catholic* they mean the RCC. The second branch is the Eastern Orthodox Church (EOC). This is a grouping of regional churches, each under the head of a Patriarch. They are sister churches of the RCC. The third branch is Protestantism. These are daughter churches of the RCC. The Reformation, starting with Martin Luther in C.E. 1517, produced many daughter (and descendent daughter) churches.

The thing that holds all three of these branches of the Catholic church together are doctrines from the Catholic creeds that were developed before the Catholic church separated into the RCC and the EOC.

163

All three hold to the creeds as being the very word of God (with some minor exceptions), and all these creeds have the word **catholic** in them. Below is the adjectival definition of *catholic*, emphases added.

1   of general scope or value; **all-inclusive; universal**
2   broad in sympathies, tastes, or understanding; liberal
3   [often C-] **of the Christian church as a whole**; specif., of the ancient, undivided Christian church
4   [C-] of the Christian church headed by the pope; Roman Catholic
5   [C-] of any of the orthodox Christian churches, including the Roman, Greek Orthodox, Anglo-Catholic, etc., as distinguished from the Reformed or Protestant churches.[1]

Protestants who use and believe the creeds take the definitions bolded above, so that when they recite the word *catholic* in the creeds, they say they mean "the universal church of the Lord Jesus Christ," and they don't capitalize it.

Historically, they—along with the dictionary—are wrong. Except for the very early church, the church always had divisions. The framers of these creeds did not mean all believers in Yahushua in whatever church they were. They called themselves *Catholic* to distinguish themselves from other Christian sects that wouldn't submit to their authority. This started in the second century, long before there was a *Roman* Catholic Church.

The early Catholic church was a network of city churches under bishops. It started going astray from the truth already in the first century. The Catholic church began with bishops who took control of churches and adopted the Roman form of government to rule. Even as the provincial capital cities ruled the cities and villages in their respective provinces, so the bishops in those capitals ruled the bishops in their respective provinces.

They did not operate as the early assembly did, each local assembly being directly under the guidance of the spirit of set-apartness. They gave themselves the name *Catholic*, and from the beginning persecuted those who wouldn't accept their authority. They claimed they were the

---

1 Webster's New World Dictionary

only true church, so of course, they would say they are Catholic. They didn't consider others as being Christian, but of being heretical sects damned to hell. Even bishops of the various Catholic churches excommunicated and damned each other to hell over differences of belief.

Catholic church spirits

Catholic church spirits are the spirits that led the assembly astray. They are very powerful demon rulers. **One of the manifestations of these Catholic church spirits is the spirit of control**. Christian organizations and groups that have this spirit damn to hell all who disagree with them. They will also do all in their power to destroy their opponents. This will be evident when we look at the Catholic creeds. The book of Revelation speaks of "Mystery, Babylon." This refers to all false religion, as well as all the world system under the devil. These creeds are part of Babylon. Elohim calls his people to come out of her (Rev. 18:4).

The "Deity" of Christ and Trinitarianism

The chief Babylon doctrine in the church is **the deity of Christ**; that is, the doctrine that says Christ existed as God before he was born. This idea started coming into the assembly as soon as it started becoming Gentile. Many doctrines came from this belief. But this doctrine is the root belief of the others, for if God is one, and Christ the Son of God is also God, then in what sense can Christ be God? This question is at the heart of the debate.

The major doctrine that came out of this belief is the doctrine of the Trinity. It started with some pagan philosophers who had converted to Christianity and became teachers and bishops in the church. The dominant pagan religion by the end of the first century was Mithraism, a religion of nature worship. It came to Rome from Persia (Iran), with some changes along the way, and was spread by Roman soldiers. Mithraism had many gods over every aspect of nature, but one god controlled them all, the one who controlled the sun and stars. His name was Mithras and he was a trinity of three gods. They were separate in name and function, but operated and were viewed as one god. Although under different names with some differences in function, this was the basic belief of all the ancient religions, all starting with Babylon. The only exception was Judaism, the belief that Elohim is one in his nature and there is no other.

In Mithraism every year, according to the cycle of nature, Mithras was born on December 25, died on Good Friday, and rose on Easter Sunday with the rising of the sun. In their belief he became a man to die for our salvation. **This was the belief of the Gentiles by the second century**. It was ingrained in their culture and was reinforced in every activity of life. When the uneducated became Christians, they had no problem in giving up their religion and believing in the one God of the Jews and in the humanity of Yahushua.

But to the Gentiles who were educated in pagan philosophy, the only way Christianity made sense was if the one God was three Persons and one of the Persons became a man while still being God. And there were three Christian names to use: Father, Son and Holy Spirit. In Mithraism the one in the middle (Mithras) was chief of the three and the other two (Cautes and Cautopates) operated at his direction, according to the cycle of the sun, from solstice to solstice.

In the picture below, Mithras is in the center with Cautes and Cautopates on either side. The cape worn by Mithras represents the universe with all the planets and stars. Cautes holds a torch facing upwards, indicating the days getting longer after the winter solstice, and Cautopates holds a torch facing downwards, indicating the days getting shorter after the summer solstice. Every aspect of the picture has pagan mythological meaning.

(Source of this picture is from the manuscript titled
"Revealing Antichrist: Exposing Mystery Babylonian Patterns
In The Historic Christian Church," author not given.)

In contrast to Mithraism, reasoned the Christians who had been edu-cated in pagan philosophy, Christianity was not a nature religion and was different from Mithraism. The difference was that all Three oper-ated all the time doing their respective responsibilities, so they must be equal. Being equal, they must have equal titles: God the Father, God the Son, and God the Holy Spirit. These titles for the Son and Holy Spirit are not in the Scriptures, but they must be true, they reasoned, for they are all equally God. So the name "Son of God" in the Scriptures means "God the Son," and the names "Spirit of God" and "holy Spirit" mean "God the Holy Spirit." (**Note:** This reasoning for the whole doctrine of the Trinity as we have it today developed and grew over several hundred years. The history of that development is not part of this book.)

As for **God the Son** becoming a man while still being God, they were used to that idea. In their pagan religion, though, the man that God became was in mythology, not a real flesh and blood human. But in Christianity Jesus *was* a real flesh and blood human. This was not a prob-lem for them, however. If God decides to become a real flesh and blood human, he can do that, for he is God and can do whatever he wants. And so God the Son became fully a human (spirit, soul and body) while still being fully God. In fact, it can only be this way, they reasoned, because only the death of God can pay for our sins. Also, in their thinking, only by God becoming a man can there be a sinless man.

It took a long time for this paganized Christian belief about Christ to be accepted by the church. The turning point was in C.E. 325 at the Council of Nicea when Emperor Constantine (the high priest of Mithraism who allegedly "converted" to Christianity) summoned certain Catholic bishops to come to an agreement on the nature of Christ. The agreement reached was that the Son of God must be fully God as the Father is God, and Constantine commanded all the bishops to sign their agreement to it or be removed from office. They also were ordered to destroy all writings that taught something different. Constantine hated Judaism and wanted nothing of it in the church, including the belief that God is one. A creed was written and came into its final form at the Council of Constantinople in C.E. 381. The purpose of the creed was to defeat the belief of Arius that Christ was a lesser god who was created by the Father God to help in creation. The belief of Arius is called Arianism, and is seen in the Jehovah's Witnesses doctrine of God today.

The Roman Catholic Church made Constantine into a saint despite his being a murderer and being the high priest of Mithraism up until his death. Keep in mind that the Christianity that Constantine converted to was a paganized form and likely he saw no fundamental difference between it and Mithraism. Constantine saw that Christianity was overtaking Mithraism as the dominant religion of the empire, and he wanted a unified empire, which meant a unified religion. After legalizing Christianity he gave it imperial favor, which resulted in many thousands of Mithraists "converting" to Christianity and many Mithraist priests becoming priests in the church. A later emperor outlawed Mithraism and other pagan religions and made Christianity the only legal religion.

Creeds

We will now look at the two most important creeds in the church, the Nicene Creed and the Athanasian Creed. The Nicene Creed began the process toward the doctrine of the Trinity by making the Son of God to be fully God as the Father is God. It is given that name because it began at the Council of Nicaea in C.E 325, and was finalized 56 years later at a later council. The Athanasian Creed was not written at any council, and it is not known how it began. It is given the name Athanasian for it began with the victory of Athanasius over Arius at the Council of Nicaea in C.E. 325. We begin with the Nicene Creed.

The Nicene Creed

The Nicene Creed (A.D. 381)

We believe in one God the Father Almighty, Maker of heaven and earth, and of all things visible and invisible.

And in one Lord Jesus Christ, the only-begotten Son of God, begotten of the Father before all worlds, God of God, Light of Light, Very God of Very God, begotten, not made, being of one substance with the Father by whom all things were made; who for us men, and for our salvation, came down from heaven, and was incarnate by the Holy Spirit of the Virgin Mary, and was made man, and was crucified also for us under Pontius Pilate. He suffered and was buried, and the third day he rose again according to the Scriptures, and ascended into heaven, and sitteth on the right hand of the Father. And he shall come again with glory to judge both the quick and the dead, whose kingdom shall have no end.

And we believe in the Holy Spirit, the Lord and Giver of Life, who proceedeth from the Father and the Son, who with the Father and the Son together is worshipped and glorified, who spoke by the prophets. And we believe one holy catholic and apostolic Church. We acknowledge one baptism for the remission of sins. And we look for the resurrection of the dead, and the life of the world to come. Amen.[2]

You may notice that this is a contradiction of terms. Why? Because what Elohim is and what man is are mutually exclusive. It takes blind faith to believe things as true that contradict each other. The following comparison illustrates the mind-bending that is necessary to believe it.

Because he was Elohim:	**But, because he was human:**
He could not sin.	He could sin.
He could not change.	He could change.
He had all knowledge.	He had limited knowledge.
He had all power.	He did not have all power.
He could do miracles.	He could not do miracles.
He could not die.	He could die.

The full deity of Christ was now established, enforced by imperial decree. Philosophers have a way of using high-sounding words that sound "spiritual," but in reality are nonsense. What does "begotten, not made" mean? "Begotten" means having a beginning, and "not made" means not having a beginning. How can the eternal Elohim become a

---

2 Source: http://www.creeds.net/ancient/nicene.htm Emphasis added. The phrase "and the Son" was a later addition to the creed.

man? In effect, he was a man by definition and in name only, not in reality, not in the way you can relate to him as a man. **Thus this doctrine, the deity of Messiah, destroys the true humanity of Yahushua**.

This creed was now the standard by which all doctrine must be tested. **It was also the standard for interpreting the Scriptures!** Today it is still the standard of all three branches of the Catholic church: Roman, Eastern Orthodox, and Protestant.

Although this became the official doctrine, it was still a battle for it to be accepted by the churches. Great protest arose against it, and it took over a hundred years before all opposition in the Catholic church was eliminated.[3] Of course, it was rejected by the non-Catholic churches, but also by many Catholic ones.

The Nicene Creed was the turning point in orthodox Catholic doctrine, paving the way for further elaboration and clarification. *Note:* **The Scriptures were no longer the final authority for the church—the Catholic councils and synods were.** The Nicene Creed raised many questions that needed answers, such as, how can Yahushua be both God and a man? Subsequent councils and synods addressed these questions, with sharp debate, each bishop seeking imperial favor for his view so as to force the others to agree. At the Council of Chalcedon in C.E. 451 they codified the idea of Jesus being both 100% human and 100% God without the mixing of the two. The final formation of the doctrine of the Trinity, however, didn't come until the Athanasian Creed.

The Athanasian Creed (C.E. 500?)

Athanasian Creed, one of the most widely used professions of faith in Western Christendom. ... The creed is a theological exposition of the doctrines of the Trinity and the incarnation, with brief statements concerning important events in the life of Jesus Christ. **The beginning and ending of the creed stress the necessity of believing the articles of faith in order to be saved.**[4]

---

3 If the apostles taught this, why did it take 200 years for it to be stated, and still there was a great fight against it?

4 Free Concise Encyclopedia Article from Encarta Online, emphasis added.

Before we go further, we need to define *incarnation.*

1a) endowment with a human body; appearance in human form

  b) Christian Theol. effectuation of the **hypostatic** union through the conception of the second person of the Trinity in the womb of the Virgin Mary

2) any person or animal serving as the embodiment of a god or spirit

3) any person or thing serving as the type or embodiment of a quality or concept [the incarnation of courage][5]

Note the definition in Christian Theology. What does "hypostatic union" mean. **It is absolute philosophical nonsense.** Yet the church calls it "holy truth." It is the foundation of the Christian faith as most of the church knows it today.

The basic meaning of "incarnation" (literally, in flesh) is "an invisible spirit becoming or living in a physical body," such as an animal or human. In Trinitarian usage it means "God who became flesh."

Incarnation also means "God who inhabited a human being." This last definition is the meaning used in this book. Although the word *incarnation* isn't in the Scriptures, the concept is, for God lived in the man Yahushua. It is recognized, however, that in Christian circles when the term "incarnation" is used, they automatically assume the Trinitarian usage of "God who became flesh." Therefore, to avoid confusion, the term "indwelling" is used. When quoting others, their words are used.

What follows is the text of the creed, brackets included by the Reformed Church, emphasis added. Hardly any of the words and concepts are from the Scriptures, and thus the whole creed is cursed (Gal 1:8-9). Yet Roman and Protestant Catholics believe God inspired this. The Eastern Orthodox branch does not accept it, although they accept parts of it. Luther accepted it because he thought it had been written before the Catholic church became Roman. Many Protestant theologians express awe at the beauty and clarity of the ideas expressed. "Only

---

5 Webster's New World Dictionary on Power CD ©1995 Zane Publishing, Inc. ©1994, 1991, 1988 Simon & Schuster, Inc., emphasis added.

God could have written such a beautiful thing," they say. As you read it, see if it "sounds" like the way Elohim inspired scripture. Emphases added.

The Athanasian Creed

Whoever wills to be in a state of salvation, before all things it is necessary that he hold the catholic [apostolic/universal] faith, which except everyone shall have kept whole and undefiled without doubt he will perish eternally.

Now the catholic faith is that **we worship One God in Trinity and Trinity in Unity**, neither confounding the Persons nor dividing the substance. For there is one Person of the Father, another of the Son, another of the Holy Spirit. But the Godhead of the Father, of the Son, and of the Holy Spirit, is One, the Glory equal, the Majesty coeternal. Such as the Father is, such is the Son, and such is the Holy Spirit; the Father uncreated, the Son uncreated, and the Holy Spirit uncreated; the Father infinite, the Son infinite, and the Holy Spirit infinite; the Father eternal, the Son eternal, and the Holy Spirit eternal. And yet not three eternals but one eternal, as also not three infinites, nor three uncreated, but one uncreated, and one infinite. So, likewise, the Father is almighty, the Son almighty, and the Holy Spirit almighty; and yet not three almighties but one almighty. So the Father is God, the Son God, and the Holy Spirit God; and yet not three Gods but one God. So the Father is Lord, the Son Lord, and the Holy Spirit Lord; and yet not three Lords but one Lord. For like as we are compelled by Christian truth to acknowledge every Person by Himself to be both God and Lord; so are we forbidden by the catholic religion to say, there be three Gods or three Lords. The Father is made of none, neither created nor begotten. The Son is of the Father alone, not made nor created but begotten. The Holy Spirit is of the Father and the Son, not made nor created nor begotten but **proceeding**. So there is one Father not three Fathers, one Son not three Sons, and one Holy Spirit not three Holy Spirits. And in this Trinity there is nothing before or after, nothing greater or less, **but the whole three Persons are coeternal together and coequal**. So that in all things, as is aforesaid, **the Trinity in Unity and the Unity in Trinity is to be worshipped. He therefore who wills to be in a state of salvation, let him think thus of the Trinity**.

But it is necessary to eternal salvation that he also believe faithfully the Incarnation of our Lord Jesus Christ. The right faith therefore is that we believe and confess that our Lord Jesus Christ, the Son of God, is God and Man. He is God of the substance of the Father begotten before the worlds, and **He is man of the substance of His mother** born in the world; perfect God, perfect man subsisting of a reasoning soul and human flesh; equal to the Father as touching His Godhead, inferior to the Father as touching His Manhood. Who although He be God and Man yet He is not two but one Christ; one however not by conversion of the Godhead in the flesh, but by taking of the Manhood in God; one altogether not by confusion of substance but by unity of Person. For as the reasoning soul and flesh is one man, so God and Man is one Christ, Who suffered for our salvation, descended into hell, rose again from the dead, ascended into heaven, sits at the right hand of the Father, from whence He shall come to judge the living and the dead. At whose coming all men shall rise again with their bodies and shall give account for their own works. And **they that have done good shall go into life eternal, and they who indeed have done evil into eternal fire**.

This is the catholic faith, which except a man shall have believed faithfully and firmly he cannot be in a state of salvation. (The Reformed Church, emphasis added.)

This is theology by definition. An example of theology by definition is like pointing to a chair and saying it is a table. Trinitarians say they are monotheists by redefining the word: "It is monotheism because we say it is, therefore it is monotheism." The whole creed, however, is pagan philosophical nonsense. That it can be believed and defended by born again believers, often fervently, shows the great power of deception that the Babylon spirits involved in it have. What follows are some comments on some of the emphasized portions.

Is eternal life by doing good? Is salvation from sin based on believing this "mystery beyond reason"? This is Gnosticism—salvation by belief in a special mystery knowledge. Do any of the salvation verses in the Scriptures (e.g. Jn 3:16; Eph 2:8-9; Rom 10:9-10) say anything like this? The apostles and prophets of the Scriptures did not teach this. Therefore this creed is cursed, along with those who teach it (Gal 1:8-9).

Many Protestant churches ignore the salvation part of this creed, saying all is true except this part. Brothers and sisters, we declare to you by the word of Elohim that the whole creed is one spirit, and the part about salvation shows what spirit it is! Just because a few scripture words are thrown in doesn't make it set-apart. This creed is poison to the human spirit; it is Babel, and Elohim wants his people to come out of it.

Pagan trinities

The list of pagan trinities below is from the manuscript "Revealing Antichrist," and it is only a sampling. All ancient religions all over the world have triads, including the Mayan, the Aztec and the Inca of Central and South America.

Beware lest anyone deceive you according to the tradition of men. (Col 2:8)

- Ra: The triple God Amun-Re, Neith, and Phtha
- Kronos: The Triad Khons
- Isis, Osiris, and Horus
- The Greek Trinity Adad
- The Sumarians Triad An, Ki and Enlil
- The Druids Trinity of Isis, Bel, and Camul
- The Persians had Ormuzd, The triple god Light, Fire, and Water

- The Chinese Sabeans Chang-ti
- The Buddhist triple goddesses god Sakya: Buddha, Dharma, and Sanga (Intelligence, Law, and Union/Harmony)
- Brahma: Brahma (the Creator), Vishnu (the Preserver), and Shiva (the Destroyer)
- The Sclavono-Vend had the triune god Triglav
- The Prussians' Perkoun, Pikollos, and Potrimpos
- The Scandinavians' Odin, Frea, and Thor
- The Etruscans' Tina, Talna, and Minerva
- The Umbrians of Iguvium Tabulae: Jou-, Mart-, and Vofi-ono-
- The triple goddess Aphrodite: The Virgin goddess, the Mother goddess, and the Crone (destroying goddess)
- Manat (origins of Islam)
- "Three fairy queens": The legend of King Arthur
- Demeter (symbolized by the genital sign of the triangle): Virgin-Mother-Crone and Creator-preserver-Destroyer
- Diana: Lunar Virgin, Mother of Creatures, and Huntress (Destroyer)
- The triple Morrigan: The Irish banshee (she-demon), or "Women of the Fairy-mounds
- The three Fates = the Norns = the Weird Sisters = the Zorya = the Morrigan = the triple Guinevere = the triple Brigit the triple goddess of past, present, and future also know as the Virgin-Mother-Crone (Creator, Preserver, Destroyer)
- The Greek triple goddesses Horae
- The three Muses
- The Graeae: (Enyo, Pemphredo, and Deino)
- The triple Moon Mother Gorgons (Medusa, Stheino, and Euryale)
- The Moerae
- The Greek goddess Fortuna: (Tyche, Dike, and Nemesis)
- The three Furies = Erinyes or Eumendides: (The Furies are said to be three personifications, representing the "vengeful moods" of the triple goddess Demeter)

All of these are from Babylon. Babylon means everything of this world which is against the ways of Elohim. This includes the idea of a trinity in God, for this is the foundation of all false religion. Although false religion began with the decision of Adam and Eve to eat fruit from the forbidden tree, as far as we can tell, the idea of God being a trinity started with Nimrod in Babylon and his attempt to build a high place. This pattern is all over the world.

Pictures of trinities

The graphic below shows that the trinity of the historic Christian church is copied from pagan trinities.

http://i34.photobucket.com/albums/d125/solarsky22/triadhs2.jpg

Below is a diagram commonly used to illustrate the Trinity. Note that it contradicts the mathematical law of reason that says things equal to the same thing must be equal to each other.

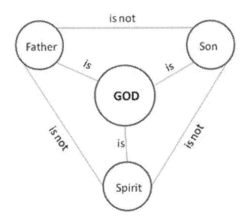

Conclusion

At the close of the last book of the Scriptures John warned against adding or taking away *"the words of the prophecy of this book"* (Rev 22:18-19). **The doctrine of three equal persons in one godhead is pagan, not scriptural.** *"Do not add to his words, lest he reprove you, and you be found a liar"* (Pr 30:6). The catholic creeds are additions to Elohim's word. Yahuah hates these creeds, and he is going to cleanse them from his temple.

There is a parallel between the idol of the trinity and the idol of the calf in the wilderness. Read Exodus 32:15-29 to see Yahuah's attitude toward idolatry, and calling that idolatry to be of him.

Moses received the Old Covenant from Elohim. While he was away with him the children of Yisra'el returned to the idolatry of Egypt (the chief elohim was a trinity), saying this idol is Elohim who had brought them out of Egypt.

Yahushua received the New Covenant from Elohim. After he went away at his ascension and started the assembly with the New Covenant, the assembly made an idol after the manner of the pagans, a trinity, and called it the god who delivered them from sin.

I love Trinitarians, but not their belief in a three-person God. Our Father is calling us to expose this idol that it may be slain in their hearts. Yahuah Elohim feels the same way about the doctrines of the "Deity" of Messiah and the Trinity as he did about that molten calf in the wilderness.

SUPPLEMENT TWO

Oneness

The doctrinal name "Oneness," as a label used for a belief about God, is the belief that "the Eternal Spirit" is one, and that the terms "Father," "Son," and "Holy Spirit" refer to three manifestations of this one Eternal Spirit. These are not Persons, but manifestations or roles only, or three ways that the Eternal Spirit reveals himself to man. An example of this oneness would be a man (one being) who has three roles, that of a husband, a father, and as an employee in a factory—three roles or manifestations, yet one being.

Although generically the term "oneness" can refer to any belief that God is one in nature and not a trinity, as used in this book the term "Oneness" refers to that specific belief only (the one defined in the paragraph above). Because thousands of Christians and hundreds of church organizations around the globe hold to this specific belief and call their belief "Oneness," that title cannot be used for the belief described in this book. In fact, there is no doctrinal label for the belief described in this book, only Scripture verses, such as *"Elohim is one"* (Gal 3:20).

The major daughter doctrine that came out of belief in the deity of Messiah is Trinitarianism. Almost the whole church worldwide is Trinitarian. In Christian books it is what defines Christianity. All general Christian bookstores are Trinitarian and they don't stock any book that is not Trinitarian, for to them, if it is not Trinitarian, it is a dangerous cult.

But belief in the deity of Messiah has another daughter doctrine that is also Christian. She is Christian because she preaches the good news as it is in the Scriptures, with the addition of believing in the deity of Messiah the same as her sister. But she believes God is one, not a trinity, and immerses in the name of Jesus. She is older than her sister Trinitarianism, but very much smaller. She calls herself Oneness. Here is the history and here is the doctrine.

By the end of the first century, before there was Trinitarianism or Oneness, there was belief among the paganized Christian philosopher bishops that the Son of God had to be deity as the Father is deity, for no one could do what he did unless he *were* deity. (Compare this idea with John 3:2.) But they also believed there is only one God. How can there be one God if both the Father and Son are deity? We have seen the Trinitarian answer: one God in three Persons. But before that answer came into being there was another answer: one God in three modes, or manifestations. They called it Modalistic Monarchianism. "Monarch" means "sole ruler," and "modal" in philosophy means "of mode, or form, as opposed to substance." This belief came into the church early in the second century.

They taught that the one God manifested himself in three forms or modes, called Father, Son and Holy Spirit. (Keep in mind that they used Greek words, not English.) It was like one actor playing three different parts by wearing three different masks (as was the custom of actors in that day). In this belief, because the Father and the Son are the same God, the Father is the Son of himself and the Son is the Father of himself. This means the Son has no separate identity from the Father. The only difference is in function.

After about a hundred years this belief almost died out. However, throughout the history of the church there have always been some Christians who maintained that God is one and not a trinity. They held widely differing beliefs as to what that meant, but the foundation belief was God is one, and one means one. After the church became solidly Trinitarian, believers in "God is one" were persecuted and often martyred by burning at the stake or other methods. (Trinitarians today still persecute Christians who don't believe in the Trinity, but not so drastically.)

As the church was being paganized by belief in the deity of Messiah, the early church experience of immersion in the spirit of set-apartness with the sign of speaking in tongues, along with miracle healing, was disappearing. Elohim was withdrawing himself from his assembly. By the time of the Council of Nicea in C.E. 325 these experiences were no longer part of the catholic church, and this sad state continued until C.E. 1901. In that year Elohim did a renewed thing. He birthed the Pentecostal movement with speaking in tongues as the sign of having received the Spirit of set-apartness, and miracle healing. Elohim was coming back to his assembly, waking his people up, and restoring lost truths from his word. This birth was among the pastors and assemblies of the "Holiness Movement." They were sick of the worldliness in the church and wanted the set-apartness (holiness) required in the Scriptures. So they were seeking the Holy Spirit. The majority of the holiness assemblies didn't accept the Pentecostal movement. In the history of the assembly, it is always the minority that are open to new things in Elohim.

When people are open to truth, Elohim gives it. And as they receive and practice it, he offers more (Mt 25:29). To these Pentecostal pastors he gave another restoration truth: **immersion in the name of Jesus**. While these Pentecostal pastors were debating "the new issue," as they called it, to those who believed it and began practicing it he gave yet another restoration truth: **God is one and one means one**. Therefore the doctrine of the Trinity is false.

Up to this point the Pentecostal pastors had agreed not to have any formal organization. And, because they realized that the Holy Spirit was moving and they didn't want to hinder receiving more revelation, they agreed to not have a statement of faith. This agreement lasted until this last-mentioned restoration truth, that **God is one and one means one.** In alarm, one of the pastors made a statement of faith that included belief in the Trinity and called a meeting of the pastors to vote on it. Two-thirds accepted it and the other third rejected it. Those of the majority who had accepted baptism in the name of Jesus lost that revelation. The majority of the two-thirds formed themselves into the Assemblies of God (AG), and the majority of the one-third formed themselves into the United Pentecostal Church (UPC).

At this point there was no name for this new restoration truth, nor even an understanding of it. And they had not received the next restoration truth, that **Yahushua is a man and man means man only**. They still believed in the deity of Jesus. To understand what this means, that God is one and Jesus is God, they went back in history to the earliest expression of this belief, before Trinitarianism; namely, Modalistic Monarchianism. But they gave it a new name: **Oneness**. In teaching, they sometimes call it "modern Oneness," to make it clear that it is not exactly the same as any of the various teachings in earlier church history. In fact, it is not clear exactly what each of the various earlier teachers taught, because we don't have their original writings. We have to go mostly by what their attackers said they taught.

The most thorough presentation of what Oneness teaches today is in the book THE ONENESS OF GOD, by David K. Bernard, J.D. © 1983, World Aflame Press. This is the publishing house of the United Pentecostal Church (UPC). (The book is on the internet. It can be found by searching for Oneness of God.)

It is not the purpose of this chapter to give a detailed commentary on Bernard's book. Rather, the purpose is to answer the question, Does Oneness teach a true humanity of Yahushua, a humanity that is the same as all other humans, except without sin? We have seen in Trinitarianism that it *says* Jesus was a true human, but because it is a humanity *different* from all other humans, it is not a *true* humanity. It is a humanity in appearance and name only.

What about Oneness? They do the same, but with a difference. In Trinitarianism, Jesus is a separate person from the Father, for they have three Persons of God. In Oneness, Jesus is both separate and the same as the Father, for they have only one person of God, except they don't use the word "person."

Here are things to note from the book. By their own confession, Jesus did not live truly as a human. A repeated theme throughout Bernard's book is that Jesus is not a human like other humans. Repeatedly they affirm his true humanity, spirit, soul and body; but repeatedly also they affirm he is different from all other humans because of his dual nature. They want it both ways. But it cannot be both ways. "Man" means "man," even as "one" means "one." Therefore, the truth is, the humanity they claim to believe in is not a true humanity.

I asked a Oneness believer, "Is Jesus human like we are human?" He answered, "No." Their emphasis is that of a "role," not that of a real human. **Even the Lamb of God in Revelation is regarded only as a**

glorified body for God the Father to manifest himself in and not a real human with a glorified body.

Trinitarian Pentecostalism flourished, and flourished more through the Charismatic or Full Gospel independent church movement. This is the fastest growing segment of the Christian church. In contrast, Oneness growth has been slow. In 2007 they had 4,358 assemblies worldwide, and over 4,000,000 members. Most Christians have never heard of them.

Elohim is the one in charge of assembly growth. Both Trinitarianism and Oneness have the deity of Christ as their foundation doctrine. Neither believe in the *true* humanity of Yahushua. Trinitarianism maintains the separate identity of the Son from the Father as a Person and gives lip service to his also being 100% human with a human body, soul and spirit. Oneness maintains that Elohim is one, but denies the separate identity of the Son from the Father. It says the human *part* of the Son is 100% human, but that part always subordinated itself to the 100% divine part. It is a mystery that can only be received by faith.

Today, another restoration truth is blowing in the assembly by the spirit of Yahuah: namely, **Yahushua Messiah is a man, and man means man only**. Only by understanding Yahushua Messiah as a *man only* can we understand the purpose of Elohim for creating man and for his desire to indwell man for eternity. The doctrine of the deity of Messiah, that Yahushua Messiah is Elohim as the Father is Elohim, whether in Trinitarianism or Oneness, completely distorts the plan of Yahuah Elohim for man, the purpose of creation, and the purpose for being born again.

Two Trinitarian Articles

The number of books and articles attempting to prove the Trinity and Deity of Christ is countless. What is given here is a sampling from two websites with refutations

Christian Apologetics & Research Ministry (www.carm.org) says, "There are cult groups ... who deny the Trinity and state that the doctrine was not mentioned until the 4th Century until after the time of the Council of Nicea (325). This council was called by Emperor Constantine to deal with the error of Arianism which was threatening the unity of the Christian Church."

The article then gives quotes from writers before the Council to supposedly "show that the doctrine of the Trinity was indeed alive-and-well before the Council of Nicea."

It is clear from a study of church history that *ideas* regarding a trinity were mentioned before 325. However, the *doctrine* of the Trinity as it is known today had its formal beginning at the council in 325, and it took hundreds of years for it to become what it is today.

There are many contradictory ideas regarding what the doctrine of the Trinity is. Their article does not state what they mean by "the doctrine of the Trinity." It appears that so long as you say, "I believe in the Trinity," then you are orthodox, even if you mean three Gods in one committee.

It is a false statement to say Emperor Constantine called the council to deal with the error of Arianism. That statement is rewriting history from a Trinitarian bias. There was no unity in the Christian Church regarding this issue. The emperor called it to deal with the division in the church regarding the nature of Christ, to force them all to believe the same. In fact, Arianism (belief that the Father created Christ to be a "god" to help him in creation) was the majority belief at the time.

Several things should be noted from the quotes CARM uses.

1) These are writings of men, not inspired Scripture, so they have no authority for doctrine.
2) The use of the words "Father, Son and Holy Spirit" do not prove a trinity, any more than the use of the names Peter, James and John do.
3) The quotes that mention the deity of Christ and a trinity show that the church strayed into paganism as quickly as the Hebrews did when they made a golden calf and called it the Elohim who brought them out of Egypt (Ex 32:4).
4) With the exception of Polycarp (who merely quoted Scripture), the writings of the men quoted in this article have many statements on other doctrines that are rejected by Christians today.

The other article for examination is *Could Christ Have Sinned* (http:// www.letusreason.org/Doct3.htm). The reasoning is: a) Man is born with a sin nature in which he cannot choose to not sin. b) God cannot sin. c) Jesus did not sin. d) Therefore Jesus is God.

Scripture rejects the idea of man having a sin nature in which he cannot choose not to sin. This is the false doctrine of Original Sin which has sent untold millions to hell: "Because I cannot help but disobey God, therefore disobeying God is okay." Man has a weakness to sin, yes, but not a sin nature. Yahushua was without sin because he chose not to sin. He was no different from his ability than Adam was when he was created. Further, if we have no choice except to sin, then Yahuah would be unjust to send us to hell for sinning.

Bibliography

Bible Dictionaries

Biblesoft's New Exhaustive Strong's Numbers and Concordance with Expanded Greek- Hebrew Dictionary. Copyright © 1994, 2003, 2006 Biblesoft, Inc. and International Bible Translators, Inc.

Easton's Bible Dictionary, PC Study Bible formatted electronic database Copyright © 2003, 2006 Biblesoft, Inc.

Exegetical Dictionary of the New Testament © 1990 by William B. Eerdmans Publishing Company (in PC Study Bible)

Explore The Book, by J.S. Baxter (in PC Study Bible)

Jamieson, Fausset, and Brown Commentary, Electronic Database. Copyright © 1997, 2003, 2005, 2006 by Biblesoft, Inc.

International Standard Bible Encyclopaedia, Electronic Database Copyright © 1996, 2003, 2006 by Biblesoft, Inc. (in PC Study Bible)

International Standard Bible Encyclopedia, revised edition, Copyright © 1979 by Wm. B. Eerdmans Publishing Co. (in PC Study Bible)

McClintock and Strong Encyclopedia, Electronic Database. Copyright © 2000, 2003, 2005, 2006 by Biblesoft, Inc.

Nelson's Illustrated Bible Dictionary, Copyright © 1986, Thomas Nelson Publishers (in PC Study Bible)

Smith's Bible Dictionary, PC Study Bible formatted electronic database Copyright © 2003, 2006 by Biblesoft, Inc.

Strong's definitions in eSword electronic database, not copyright

Strong's Exhaustive Bible Concordance with Greek and Hebrew Lexicon (not copyright)

Thayer's Greek Lexicon, Electronic Database. Copyright © 2000, 2003, 2006 by Biblesoft, Inc.

The Complete Word Study Dictionary: New Testament Copyright © 1992 by AMG International, Inc. Revised Edition, 1993

The Complete Word Study Dictionary: Old Testament Copyright © 2003 by AMG Publishers. All rights reserved.

The New Unger's Bible Dictionary. Originally published by Moody Press of Chicago, Illinois. Copyright © 1988.

Theological Dictionary of the New Testament (TDNT), abridged edition, Copyright © 1985 by William B. Eerdmans Publishing Company. All rights reserved.

Theological Wordbook of the Old Testament. Copyright © 1980 by The Moody Bible Institute of Chicago. All rights reserved

United Bible Societies definitions in BibleWorks electronic database, not copyright.

Vine's Expository Dictionary of Biblical Words, Copyright © 1985, Thomas Nelson Publishers. All rights reserved.

Wheeler's Greek Syntax Notes, Copyright © 1985-2002 by Rev. Dale M. Wheeler, Ph.D. All rights reserved. Used by Permission. (In Biblesoft)

Bible Translations

Interlinear Transliterated Bible. Copyright © 1994, 2003 by Biblesoft, Inc. All rights reserved.

The King James Version (KJV), Electronic Database Published by Biblesoft.

Holman Christian Standard Bible® (HCSB) Copyright © 1999, 2000, 2002, 2003, 2005 by Holman Bible Publishers. All rights reserved.

The New American Standard Bible (NAS), in Bibleworks database.

The New American Standard Bible Update (NASU). Copyright © 1960, 1962, 1963, 1968, 1971, 1972, 1973, 1975, 1977, 1995, by The Lockman Foundation. Used by permission. All rights reserved.

The New King James Version (NKJV), Copyright © 1982, Thomas Nelson, Inc. All rights reserved.

The New International Version (NIV), Published by International Bible Society, in Biblesoft. Used by permission.

New Revised Standard Version (NRSV) Copyright © 1989 Division of Christian Education of the National Council of the Churches of Christ in the United States of America. Used by permission. All rights reserved.

The Living Bible (TLB) Copyright © 1971. Used by permission of Tyndale House Publishers, Inc., Wheaton, IL. All rights reserved.

The Scriptures (TS). Copyright © 2000 by Institute for Scripture Research (Pty) Ltd. Northriding, Republic of South Africa. Used by permission.

Books

Come Out of Her My People. By C. J. Koster. Institute for Scripture Research, Northriding, Republic of South Africa. Strawberry Islands Messianic Publishing, Louisville, Kentucky. © Copyright 2004 by Institute for Scripture Research (Pty) Ltd.

Fossilized Customs—The Pagan Sources of Popular Customs. By Lew White. 5th Edition. Strawberry Islands Messianic Publishing, Louisville, Kentucky.

Jesus Salvation & The Rapture—The Truth About Christianity. By David Kirke, Copyright © 1998 Kirke Ministries, Pub. by: Kirke Ministries, Seahurst, WA, an imprint of: Champions Publishing.

New Light on the Difficult Words of Jesus—Insights from His Jewish Context. By David Bivin. Copyright © 2005 by David Bivin. Published by the En-Gedi Resource Center, Inc., Holland, Michigan.

One God & One Lord—Reconsidering the Cornerstone of the Christian Faith. By Mark H. Graeser, John A. Lynn and John W. Schoenheit. Published by Christian Educational Services, Inc., Indianapolis, Indiana, Second Edition ©2000, all rights reserved.

Systematic Theology. By Charles G. Finney, Ed. by J.H. Fairchild 1878 President, Oberlin college 1878 EDITION (from Systematic Theology, Electronic Database Copyright ©1999 by Biblesoft)

The Apostolic Fathers, Translated and Edited by J. B. Lightfoot, Baker Book House, Grand Rapids, Michigan, Sixth Printing,

1971. This English translation of *The Apostolic Fathers* is reprinted from the edition published in 1891 by Macmillan and Company, London.

The Hebrew Yeshua vs. the Greek Jesus. By Nehemia Gordon. Hilkiah Press, 2006, Copyright © by Nehemia Gordon. All rights reserved.

The History of Christian Doctrines. By Louis Berkhof. Baker Book House, Grand Rapids, Michigan. © Copyright 1937 by Louis Berkhof.

The Names of God, by Nathan Stone, Copyright © 1944 by the Moody Bible Institute of Chicago.

Understanding the Difficult Words of Jesus—New Insights From a Hebraic Perspective. By David Bivin and Roy Glizzard, Jr., Revised Edition. ©1983, 1984 by David Bivin and Roy Blizzard, Jr. ©1994 Revised Edition. Published by Destiny Image® Publishers, Inc. Shippensburg, Pennsylvania.

Yeshua—A Guide to the Real Jesus and the Original Church. By Dr. Ron Moseley. Lederer Books a division of Messianic Jewish Publishers, Clarksville, Maryland. Copyright © 1996 by Ronald Wayne Mosely. All rights reserved.

Booklets and Pamphlets

22 Principles of Bible Interpretation —or—How to Eliminate Apparent Bible Contradictions. Christian Educational Services, Indianapolis, Indiana. (http://stfonlinestore.com/booklets.aspx)

34 Reasons Why The Holy Spirit Is Not A Separate "Person" From The Only True God, The Father. Christian Educational Services, Indianapolis, Indiana. (http://stfonlinestore.com/booklets.aspx)

46 Reasons Why Our Heavenly Father Has No Equals, Or "Co-Equals." Christian Educational Services, Indianapolis, Indiana. (http://stfon-linestore.com/booklets.aspx)

God In Man—God's Plan of Incarnation. By Gilbert W. Olson. Copyright © 1995 by Gilbert W. Olson. All rights reserved.

History & Christianity. By John Warwick Montgomery, InterVarsity Press, Downers Grove, Illinois, ©1964 and 1965 by Inter-Varsity Christian Fellowship of the United States of America, All rights reserved.

One God: The Father of Jesus Christ. By Robert Carden. Grace Christian Fellowship, Naperville, Illinois.

Should You Believe in the Trinity? (No author or publisher given, but published by Watch Tower.)

The Eternal Sonship—A refutation according to Adam Clarke. By David Campbell, ©1978 Word Aflame® Press, Hazelwood, Mo.

World Religions Made Easy. Hendrickson Publishers, Inc., Peabody, Massachusetts. Copyright ©1999 John Hunt.

Commentaries

Adam Clarke's Commentary, Electronic Database. Copyright © 1996, 2003, 2005, 2006 by Biblesoft, Inc.

Barnes' Notes, Electronic Database. Copyright © 1997, 2003, 2005, 2006 by Biblesoft, Inc.

Jamieson, Fausset and Brown Commentary (JFB), General Domain, in Biblesoft.

Keil & Delitzsch Commentary On The Old Testament New Updated Edition Electronic Database. Copyright © 1996 by Hendrickson Publishers, Inc.

Other

Blitz, Mark, "The Feasts of the Lord" (4DVD+1 series, incl. a manual), El Shaddai Ministries.

Challis, Tim (Associate pastor of Grace Fellowship Church, Toronto, Ontario, Canada) "What Kind of God Would Condemn People to Eternal Torment," Answers Magazine, Vol. 7 No. 3 July-Sept. 2012, p.58.

Collins English Dictionary – Complete and Unabridged © HarperCollins Publishers 1991, 1994, 1998, 2000, 2003.

Random House Webster's Unabridged Dictionary on CD Rom

Random House Kernerman Webster's College Dictionary, © 2010 K Dictionaries Ltd. Copyright 2005, 1997, 1991 by Random House, Inc. All rights reserved.

The American Heritage® Dictionary of the English Language, Fourth Edition copyright ©2000 by Houghton Mifflin Company. Updated in 2009. All rights reserved.

The Sage's English Dictionary and Thesaurus, Sequence Publishing, free download.

Webster's Revised Unabridged Dictionary, published 1913 by C. & G. Merriam Co.

Websites

Could Christ Have Sinned. http://www.letusreason.org/Doct3.htm.

Davies-Kildea, Jason, Boundless Salvation. http://boundless-salvation. blogspot.com/2008/10/immanenceimminence-of-god.html.

Deity of Jesus Christ. http://www.abideinchrist.com/keys/deity.html.

Early Trinitarian Quotes. www.carm.org.

Is Trinitarianism Monotheistic? by Kermit Zarley. http://www.patheos. com/blogs/kermitzarleyblog/2013/05/is-trinitarianism-monotheistic/.

Father's Name Made Simple – Yahuah www.yahuahreigns.com/ FathersName.

Holy Spirit (Judaism). http://en.wikipedia.org/wiki/Holy_Spirit_(Judaism).

How God Conceived Jesus in Mary's Womb, by Craig Bluemel. http:// www.bibleanswerstand.org/conceived.htm.

Is the Creators name spelled Yahuah or Yahuwah? by Lamadyahu. http://m.youtube.com/#/watch?v=1TUFHWR4SHE&desktop_ uri=%2Fwatch%3Fv%3D1TUFHWR4SHE.

Jesus Is Not The Father, So how can he be God? http://www.letusrea-son.org/Trin6.htm.

Judaism 101. Messiah: The Messiah, by Tracey R Rich. http://www.jew-faq.org/Messiah.htm.

Kirke. www.theoi.com/Titan/Kirke.html.

Merriam-Webster Dictionary. m-w.com.

Nazarenes and the Name of YHWH. www.nazarene.net/_halacha/ Nazarenes_and_the_name.

Proofs For Jesus Being Deity. http://www.letusreason.org/Trin12.htm.

ProsperityTheology.http://en.wikipedia.org/wiki/Prosperity_theology.

Ruach Studies by Paul Sumner. http://www.hebrew-streams.org/works/ spirit/ruachpneuma.html.

The Alphabet of Biblical Hebrew. http://biblescripture.net/Hebrew. html.

The Basics of Light. http://violet.pha.jhu.edu/~wpb/spectroscopy/ basics.html.

The Name of God: Jewish Virtual Library. www.jewishvirtuallibrary. org/jsource/Judaism/name.html © 2012 The American-Israeli Cooperative Enterprise.

The Names of God. By J. Hampton Keathley, III. http://bible.org/ article/names-god.

The Names of God in the Old Testament. http://www.blueletterbible. org/study/misc/name_god.cfm#link7.

The Omniscience of God, by Caleb Colley, M.L.A. http://www.apologet- icspress.org.

The Omniscience of God: Does the Lord Really Know Everything? By Joe Nesom, http://www.founders.org/journal/fj46/article1.html.

The Problem of Evil. http://www.catholiceducation.org/articles/reli- gion/re0019.html.

The True Pronunciation of the Sacred Name, Hope of Israel Ministries. www.hope-of-israel.org.

Was Jesus Sinless and Does It Matter. http://www.toughquestionsan- swered.org/2013/03/11/was-jesus-sinless-and-does-it-matter/.

Wiki Answers. http://wiki.answers.com.

Wikipedia, the free encyclopedia.

About The Author

Gilbert Olson was born in Seattle, Washington in 1934, the fourth of five boys. At 13 years of age he received Yahushua as his Savior and Master, and when 18 heard the call from the Father to be a missionary in Africa.

With his wife, Beverly, he served as a pastor in America (8 years), as a missionary in Sierra Leone, West Africa (11 years) and in the Philippines (13 years). As a missionary his main responsibility was training pastors and church leaders. In 2005 he became the Academic Dean of House of David Scripture College in Boise, Idaho and prepared most of the teaching materials. He retired from that position in 2014, but still teaches.

He holds the following degrees:

B.A. in Religion, Seattle Pacific University, Seattle, WA

B.D., United Theological Seminary, Dayton, OH

M.A. in Missions, Fuller Theological Seminary, Pasadena, CA

B.Th., Pacific School of Religion, Burien, WA

M.Min. (Master of Ministry), Pacific School of Religion

D.Th., House of David Scripture College, Boise, ID

Books published:

"Church Growth in Sierra Leone." Part of the Church Growth series of the School of World Mission.

"God In Man—God's Plan of Incarnation."

Gilbert and his wife, Beverly, live in Meridian, Idaho.

Made in the USA
Lexington, KY
17 January 2018